how to retire and not die

THE 3 Ps
THAT WILL KEEP
YOU YOUNG

GARY SIRAK

WITH MAX SIRAK

Copyright © 2021 Gary Sirak with Max Sirak

How to Retire and Not Die:
The 3 Ps That Will Keep You Young

Hardcover ISBN: 978-1-5445-2374-3
Paperback ISBN: 978-1-5445-2372-9
eBook ISBN: 978-1-5445-2373-6
Audiobook ISBN: 978-1-5445-2247-0

*This book is dedicated to anyone
approaching retirement, or who is retired,
and trying to figure this out.*

The stories you're about to read are true. And, like I learned from Sergeant Joe Friday when I was a kid, I changed names to protect the innocent.

CONTENTS

INTRODUCTION

WELCOME TO MY WORLD!
My name is Gary Sirak and I've spent forty years working as a financial advisor helping my clients prepare for retirement. And, for the last ten years, I've been writing books. This is my third.

My first book, *If Your Money Talked What Secrets Would it Tell*, is my spin on personal finance. It's about how money works and how to manage it. *The American Dream Revisited* is my second. It's about how people worked hard, sought help, and achieved their dreams. You can find these and more at garysirak.com.

Before going any further, you and I need to get crystal clear. This book, *How To Retire and Not Die: The 3 Ps That Will Keep You Young*, is NOT about how to accumulate money for retirement or how to manage your assets if you're already retired. Nope. This book is all about how to find happiness and success during your retirement years.

Unfortunately, very few people I've worked with are truly prepared for retirement. They assume money is the only thing that matters and stop there. Almost no one has good answers to the questions, "What are you going to do with your time? How are you going to spend the rest of your life?"

Think about it. Let's say you retire at age 65. I'm no actuary, but most of my personal clients have lived well into their 80s. That means you're going to be on the hook for filling some serious time.

Retirement isn't a sprint. Retirement is a marathon. A marathon you climbed a mountain in order to get to. Let me explain.

THE MOUNTAIN AND THE MARATHON

When I was in my twenties, I had the pleasure of spending a month hiking in Grand Teton National Park in Wyoming. The scenery was spectacular. The stars in the night sky even more so. And the sense of accomplishment that came from getting to the top of those peaks and enjoying the breath-taking vistas was life-changing.

But getting there? That was a very different story. Descriptive words like brutal, daunting, exhausting, and blistering come to mind.

Make no mistake, the views were worth it. I wouldn't trade them for the world, but they were also earned step by sometimes excruciating step. And that doesn't even count the way-too-close-for-comfort encounter with a family of bears, or the run-in with the moose that was bigger than the car we drove across the country.

So, how does my time in the Tetons relate? There is a similarity between my experience getting to the top of the mountains and your experience getting to retirement. Both were climbs. Though, hopefully, only one of ours involved bears and a moose.

Neither of us moved in a straight line. For my climb in the mountains, this was due to steepness. For you, getting to retirement, the twists and turns of life, family, and careers had you zigzagging to the top.

We both had to earn it. You through blood, sweat, and tears. Me, mostly through blisters, sweat, and fears. Have I mentioned I don't much like heights?

And, just like me, you made it. That's no small feat. Just finishing the climb to retirement is one hell of an accomplishment. I mean it. Congratulations are in order.

Now, here's where our stories diverge. Because for me, after I made it to the top of my mountain, I had it easy. All I had to do was take a load off, take a breather, take in the view, and take my time getting back down to camp.

You, on the other hand, have it much tougher. All your hard work and effort to make it to the top of your mountain, retirement, has a different reward—a marathon.

That's right. Your climb to get to retirement was just the first part of your journey. And, as soon as you get there, it's time to start the second part—your marathon.

It's not a marathon you have to run. It's the one you get to live.

Why do I call the rest of your life after you a retire a marathon? Simple math. Say you retire at 65 and live longer than my average client, to age 91. That's 26 years of life after work, the same number of miles in a marathon.

WHO THIS BOOK IS FOR

This book is a guide for people who are, or are about to, start living their marathon. It's for the people who have already made it to the top of the mountain and now find themselves lacing up their shoes to take the first steps of the rest of their lives.

WHO THIS BOOK ISN'T FOR

People climbing the mountain. If you want a book telling you how to get to the marathon, you, my friend, are in the wrong place.

This might not come as a shock, but in my experience, the first words out of anyone's mouth when talking about retirement are about dollars and cents. "Do I have enough?" "How can I make sure it lasts?" "Will I still get to take vacations or buy my dream car?" Etc.

It's not that money questions aren't important. They are. But you won't find the answers to those questions in this book.

Just to be clear, if it's the money aspect of retirement you're focused on, I've got news for you. You're going to be severely disappointed. Do us both a favor and put this book right back where you found it. It'll save you some time and me some bad reviews.

Instead, find yourself a trusted financial advisor, or read one of the other countless books that discuss getting to retirement. Then, when you find yourself at, or near the top of the mountain, by all means, pick this book up again.

HOW TO USE THIS BOOK

I've done my best to put everything I've learned about retiring and not dying into a system that makes sense, is easy to use, and fun to read. At least, that's my hope.

The book is broken up into three parts. Part 1 lays the foundation. Part 2 introduces you to the exercises and Tools. Part 3 walks you through building the right retirement for you.

I encourage you to take your time with the parts of this book that ask you to do a bit of self-reflection, or navel gazing, as an old professor of mine used to say. You'll know these parts when you see them. Because while I've cataloged the general similarities between the different, happy retired people I've met, the specifics range wildly. And it's those specifics, unique to each person and their lives, that make all the difference.

Building the right retirement for you means knowing yourself. I say "right for you" because retirement isn't one-size fits all. It's more made to order and tailored to fit.

Getting to know yourself is the only shot you have at getting retirement right.

WHY DID I WRITE THIS? AND WHY SHOULD YOU READ THIS?

Ah, yes. Turn the page. There are some stories I'd like to share to answer these two important questions…

CHAPTER 1

The "Whys"

WHY DID I WRITE this book?
That I'll answer with two stories.

GETTING IT WRONG

Early in my career, I sat in on an appointment with my father, Stan, who founded Sirak Financial Services in 1957. To say this appointment was memorable doesn't begin to scratch the surface. It's where the seed for this book was first planted.

My father had known his clients, Bruno and Betty, since high school. The three of them were close friends and they were meeting to celebrate. Bruno was retiring.

It was a lunchtime appointment. I remember being slightly confused as my father and I pulled up to a very non-descript house on the south end of Canton, Ohio. Imagine my surprise when what I assumed to just be a normal home turned out to be a private dining club.

This place was so fancy, there wasn't even a menu. Delicious food, enough for a small army, continued to appear throughout the entire meeting. I was in awe. It was the best (and the most) Italian food I'd ever eaten. To this day, it remains in the top five dining experiences of my life.

Bruno, as I mentioned, was retiring. He had invented, patented, and manufactured an automotive part that the Big Three used in all their cars. A competitor of his offered to buy his whole operation for $10 million—a staggering amount of money in the 1980s.

During our two-hour lunch, the conversation shifted from the nuts and bolts of the deal to Bruno retiring.

Dad asked him what seemed like a pretty simple question, "What's next? What are you going to do with the remaining years of your life?"

Bruno shrugged. "Betty and I are going to Italy for a month to visit family," he said.

"That's great," replied my dad, "but that's only one month. I want to know—what are you going to do with the rest of your life?"

At this point, Betty chimed in. "All you've ever done is work. You don't take days off. You don't have any hobbies. You spend almost every waking hour at the shop. I'm worried about you."

"Bah, I'll figure it out," scoffed Bruno. "There's nothing to worry about."

"Betty's right," said Dad. "This retirement thing, it isn't a walk in the park. You need to have a plan."

"Plan?" laughed Bruno. "C'mon Stan, you know me. I've got plenty of time and money. I'll do what I always do. I'll figure it out."

With that, perfectly punctuating the finality of Bruno's statement, three waiters waltzed into the room. Each carried a tray loaded with different desserts. Like I said, one of my top five dining experiences.

As soon as we got back into the car, I began raving. "That was one of the best meals of my life. Thank you for inviting me along, Dad. Did you try the lasagna? What about the tiramisu? I didn't even know I liked tiramisu."

A few seconds passed. He hadn't replied so I glanced over. My father was scowling, lost in deep thought. "What's wrong?" I asked.

After a heavy sigh, he answered. "Bruno's lack of planning is going to lead to bad things. You heard Betty. All he does is work. It's his passion. It's his purpose. And he's about to lose them, and that's not good."

"Passion? Purpose? Who needs those when You've got 10 million bucks?"

"Everyone. Gary, it's not about money and it never will be. If Bruno doesn't figure out what he's going to do with the rest of his life, then all the money in the world won't mean a thing. You and I will be at his funeral before you know it."

Sadly, Bruno never figured it out.

My dad and I attended his funeral less than two years later.

GETTING IT RIGHT

Simone, a retired physician, and her husband, Larry, came to see me for their annual financial review. Simone was a good saver during her professional life. So much so, she had retired twelve years earlier, at the age of 60.

"You've been at this retirement game for a while, Simone. How have you managed to stay busy after all these years?" I asked.

"Oh, you know. A little of this. A little of that," she said.

Larry laughed. "Gary, don't let her fool you. She had a plan. I had no idea she had so many interests and I've been married to her for forty years," he said. "She manages our finances, plans our vacations, and is amazing in the kitchen. Look at me. I've put on ten pounds!"

"I've always been a planner," added Simone. "Retirement was no different. I have a regular Pilates class. I do yoga twice a week at the YMCA. I walk the dog every day and volunteer at a wellness clinic. Nothing too crazy or stressful."

"She's being modest, Gary. There's more."

Simone smiled. "He's right. I golf a few times a week in a league. When the weather isn't nice, I meet my friends for coffee or lunch. I'm as busy as I want to be. I enjoy my life."

"I've got to admit, Simone, you do seem genuinely happy," I said. "Actually, you're one of the happiest retired people I know."

"Thanks, Gary! I guess early on in the process I made up my mind that I was going to spend the rest of my life doing what made me happy. I'd spent so many years doing things for others, I decided this part of my life was going to be about doing things for me...and Larry, of course. As long as he wants to do the things I want to do."

She looked over at Larry and smiled.

Simone is a perfect example of successful retirement— her attitude and approach are the foundation of what a successful retirement looks like. She varies her activities. Her schedule gives her structure. She engages socially. Most importantly, she's happy and enjoys her life.

I wrote this book because I want to help you get retirement right. The way I see it, you have two choices. You can be like Bruno and barely get out of the starting gate, or be like Simone, who is cruising through, living her marathon.

WHY YOU SHOULD READ THIS

You should read this so you can live your marathon and stay young! You're reading my book because you're about to retire, or already have, and would prefer to stick around a while longer. That's a good goal. One I think I can help you with.

I'm guessing you didn't climb the mountain to retirement to live out your days in boredom and misery. Call it a hunch. No. You want a successful, happy, and hopefully long retirement, right?

Before going any further, there's something you need to understand. As I mentioned, a "successful" and "happy" retirement isn't one-size fits all. Not even close. The retirement of my dreams might sound like a nightmare to you.

This is the point—your retirement doesn't have to look like your parents', your neighbors', your friends', or mine. All that matters is that it works for you.

Now, that said, if we were painting with watercolors in the broadest strokes here, we could say everyone wants the same things out of their retirement: increased freedom and more enjoyment.

Increasing your freedom is pretty self-explanatory. It's the ability to do what you want when you want.

Increasing enjoyment means maintaining or elevating your current lifestyle.

Here's the thing. Retiring produces a huge windfall of your most precious resource: time. But it's a resource you might not be the best at managing. With more time on your hands, you have the opportunity to spend it in meaningful and fulfilling ways. This book can help you do that.

INSIGHTS

My father was very smart. He knew there were three things everyone needed in retirement: Passion, Purpose, and a Plan. These are the 3 Ps that will keep you young, and help you retire and not die.

You can listen to my father's advice or ignore it and see what happens.

You probably know someone who didn't. They retired, ignored the 3 Ps, and well, you know how their story ended. I'm guessing too quickly and with too many tears.

Maybe you're thinking to yourself, "What? You don't know me. I'm different. That won't happen. I've been working my whole life, waiting for this moment. I'm going to be fine. I'll be free to do whatever I want."

You're right. I probably don't know you. But what I do know is you've worked very hard your whole life, climbing the mountain to get to this point. And I also know what I've seen. People who don't have a Plan don't seem to last very long. Which brings us back to the reason you're holding this book.

You are reading this because you want to know how to retire, be happy, feel successful, and enjoy living your marathon.

Lucky for you, I've had a lot of experience with retirement. I've seen what works and what doesn't. Which means I'm in the unique position of being able to help.

Now that we're on the same page, it's off to the races. Remember, retirement is a marathon. And since no one in their right mind would decide to run one of those without a little bit of preparation and training, it's time to get to work.

Specifically, groundwork.

PART 1

PART I

CHAPTER 2

Groundwork

I F YOU'RE READING THIS, it means you've decided to be like Simone, and I'm glad you did.

As I mentioned, Part 1 is about laying down the proper foundation. While it's true, as I have explained, retirement is much more a marathon than a sprint. Building a happy, successful, and hopefully long-lived retirement is just that: building.

And, if you've ever built anything before, you know one of the first steps is preparing the surface you're going to build on. If you don't take the time to smooth it out and clear away debris, then there's a pretty good chance what you're planning to build won't be right. At best, it'll be crooked and lopsided. At worst, it won't even stand.

(This is how it usually goes for me, which is why "Building things" is one of my Hates. Don't worry. This will make way more sense once we get to Part 2...)

This section of the book is about laying down the proper foundation. We're going to take some time and cover the things that will become the bedrock of your 3 Ps: Passion, Purpose, and Plan. We'll start with a little history and then take time to explore some beliefs and ideas about retirement. After that, it's a slight detour as we wind back and think a bit more deeply about work, before finally finishing off with a discussion about mindset.

That way, when I introduce you to the Tools you're going to use (Part 2) to build your Plan (Part 3), you'll have a nice, solid, stable base to work from.

Sound good?

Great.

Let's dig into some groundwork!

CHAPTER 3

How We Got Here

WHERE BETTER TO START than at the beginning?
I don't read a lot of science fiction these days. I'm more of a mystery-thriller kind of guy, but one of my favorite sci/fi authors is Terry Pratchett. He's a marvelous storyteller with a knack for mixing just the right amounts of wit and wisdom into his tales to ensure they go down smoothly.

Here. Take a sip from *I Shall Wear Midnight* and see for yourself. Tell me, is there a better way to start a chapter about the history of something? I don't know of one.

"If you do not know where you come from, then you don't know where you are, and if you don't know where you are, then you don't know where you're going."

So, I'd like to spend a little bit of time talking about how we got to where we are. I know. You're excited. You want to start building and living the happy and successful retirement of your dreams right now. Today. And, I promise, that is

100 percent where we are going. However, the first step we need to take, as Terry tells us, involves going back, and that is exactly what we are going to do.

SALT MONEY AND PENSIONS

The idea of caring for the older members of society goes back a long way. Really long. Like ancient Rome long. Retirement, like the word salary, owes its roots to Rome. If a soldier was lucky enough to live through their campaigns of service, they were then entitled to a portion of their previous "salt money" or, salary, when they returned home. This is one of the first examples of a retirement pension.

Fast forward a couple thousand years, and it's still the military we point to for the origins of pensions in the United States. During the Revolutionary War, one of the ways men were encouraged to sign up for service was by offering them guaranteed money for the rest of their lives. The catch here, again, is they had to live through the war.

It didn't take the private sector much longer to begin exploring the idea of pensions. In 1875, American Express was one of the first companies to venture down this road. According to the Bureau of Labor Statistics, after twenty years of service and upon reaching the age of 60, workers were entitled to half their salary until the day they died.

The remaining half of their salary was then used to hire a new employee to replace the recently retired one. Those who were newest to the workforce were willing to work for less. This method of worker replacement created a healthy flow of employees for American Express.

Because this system worked so well, other companies hopped onboard. By the turn of the twentieth century, railroads, steel, oil, and all the big industries of the time began offering pensions.

SOCIAL SECURITY

Social Security, the idea of nations caring for the aging population, has also been around for a while. Maybe not quite as long as pensions and salaries, but still hundreds of years. Some historians trace the idea all the way back to the artisan guilds of the Middle Ages.

In the United States, however, the story of Social Security is much more recent. It begins with the Great Depression. Over a three-month period, the stock market tanked 40 percent and lost $26 billion. Unemployment skyrocketed to 25 percent, and more than 10,000 banks defaulted and failed. As a result, the poverty rates of the elderly population ballooned to around 50 percent.

All of this prompted Franklin Delano Roosevelt to sign the Social Security Act of 1935. The Act outlined a system based on a model Otto von Bismarck, Imperial Chancellor of Prussia, tried in the 1880s. It was a social insurance program that workers paid *into* while employed, and were then entitled to take benefits *out of* when they reached a certain age.

The age has changed with time. When I started my career, 65 was the magic number for retirement because that was when you received full benefits. Now, the magic age has crept up a bit. For example, if you were born after 1960, your full benefits won't kick in until you're 67 years old.

401(K)S

As hard as this may be to believe, 401(k)s have only been around since 1980, and they only came to be by accident. They were the byproduct of the Revenue Act of 1978. The name itself, 401(k), refers to a specific section of the tax code.

The story goes, Ted Benna, a consultant for an insurance brokerage firm, came up with the idea of a 401(k). He was trying to help a client streamline their retirement costs and pitched them his new concept. And, as often happens with new ways of doing things, the client rejected his proposal.

However, about a year later, 401(k)s really got rolling. The IRS began allowing employees to deduct their contributions directly from their paychecks. Within two years, a substantial number of major companies made the switch from pensions to employee-funded plans with matches, a.k.a. 401(k)s. And, as of today, pensions have all but vanished.

AND SO THIS LEAVES US WHERE, EXACTLY?

Now that you have a sense of how we got here, let's talk about where "here" is.

According to a Pew Research study, 10,000 people per day turn 65 in the United States. Sixty-five is still a popular age when people begin to claim their Social Security benefit. This means more people are drawing on Social Security today than in any point in history.

In 1937, two years after the Social Security Act was signed into law, 53,000 people were collecting. As of August 2020, the Center on Budget and Policy Priorities reported the number of people collecting benefits at 64,000,000.

Then, there's the fact we live a lot longer now. Thanks to advances in medicine, life expectancy in the United States is now projected to be around 79 years. This means not only are more people collecting Social Security than ever before, but they're doing it for a longer period of time.

INSIGHTS

From ancient Rome, through the Great Depression, and up to today—that was my Reader's Digest version of the history of retirement.

Lucky for us, I'm not a historian. My job isn't to teach about what was, my job is to help you get to where you want to be—living the marathon of your happy, successful, retired life.

And, like Mr. Pratchett said it's now with a better understanding of how we got to where we are, that we will be better equipped to think about where we want to go. Our next step on this journey of how to retire, not die, and stay young concerns the concept of retirement itself.

Have you ever taken a moment to question the idea of retirement, why we do it, or if it's even good for us?

CHAPTER 4

Why You Think You Should Retire

RETIREMENT, LIKE PRETTY MUCH everything else in this life, can be either good or bad. I've seen some people, like Simone, wear it really well and make it look good. Others, like Bruno, not so much. The reality is, some people are happier working than not. Which is why the first question I ask anyone I meet who wants to talk retirement is:

"Why do you want to retire?"

And believe me when I tell you, the answers I've gotten back are something else. So much so I started keeping a list. Below are a handful of my favorites. Some make sense. Some make me smile. Some make me laugh.

All I do all day is stare at my computer screen. It's killing my vision.

I'm on my feet the whole day.

They don't allow naps.

My boss is half my age and she's got tattoos. I thought about getting one just to fit in, but my wife told me if I did I'd have to sleep in a different room.

I can't keep up with the new technology. We installed a new computer system that required training and it was just easier to retire.

I'm tired of winter.

My grandchildren are growing up and I want to spend time with them.

The company is downsizing and made me an offer I couldn't refuse.

I'm a lifetime baseball fan and my wife and I are going to travel to all the ballparks in the country.

I'm just tired of working. It's not fun anymore. All they want to do is make money.

The new owners don't appreciate my knowledge and expertise.

I'm determined to make the PGA Seniors Tour.

My friends are all doing it and I don't want to be left out.

By my count, there are a number of reasons, but they all fit into three main categories: physical, mental, and social.

PHYSICAL

Aging is the most obvious physical reason people want to retire. As basketball great LeBron James says, "Father Time is undefeated." And, depending on the job, aging can show up in different ways.

Take Pierce for example. Pierce is a friend of mine who laid bricks starting at an early age. From the time he was sixteen, he worked six days a week and made good money doing it. Then, at the age of fifty-five the physical toll from thirty-nine years of masonry caught up to him. Here's what he said about it:

"Gary, you know? It was a pretty easy decision. I woke up one morning and I couldn't get out of bed."

Nina's story is different. She is a client of mine who used to work as the office manager for a large chain of auto dealerships. This meant she spent forty plus hours per week dealing with numbers and staring at computer screens.

The money was great. She enjoyed what she did and she was good at it. Not to mention, in her words, "It's not like driving a new car every year hurt, either." But, despite how much Nina loved her job and the life it gave her, there was one huge problem.

Nina was losing her vision. And the more time she spent straining to make sense of the numbers on her printouts and screens, the worse it got. By the time she turned 60, she was no longer able to do her job.

MENTAL

There's no question the mental demands of work can also be a reason to retire.

A physician friend of mine, John, recently made the difficult decision of shuttering his practice. The stress of running a business finally got the best of him. Listen to how he tells it:

"Gary, I was in the office one afternoon, trying to catch up on paperwork and feeling exhausted. I'd spent the better part of the last year frustrated with the transition from hand-written charts to electronic medical records. It was cutting into my time and taking me away from the whole reason I became a doctor, caring for patients."

"What tipped you over the edge, John?"

"I scheduled a physical for myself with my doc. He took one look at my blood pressure and told me it was too high.

He gave me the options of going on meds or reducing the stress in my life. With that information in mind, I decided to retire."

SOCIAL

There are plenty of social reasons that cause us to want to retire.

What you witnessed growing up probably influenced you greatly. Your parents and grandparents created a blueprint, a virtual model of what work and retirement was supposed to look like. So, now that you find yourself at a similar place in time, it's only natural for you to refer to the retirement road map you were given.

If you watched your parents and/or grandparents retire at 65, then retiring at 65 is likely what you expect.

Social Security is another cue. Retiring as soon as you can collect your benefits is deeply ingrained in the American psyche. A significant amount of the population views this national social insurance policy as the top of the mountain. Once they get there, the climb is over. They've won. It's time to quit and smell the roses.

Watching the people you care about and love getting older is another reason. Let's face it. Time is our most precious resource. It's limited and most people reach a certain point where they stop wanting to trade it for money.

INSIGHTS

There are plenty of good reasons to retire. There are also plenty of bad ones. The point is, retirement is not one size fits all. Whether or not it's good for you depends on who you are and how you do it.

Being honest with yourself about why you're retiring is a really good first step. The next step after that is determining if you're the type of person who's genuinely happiest when working. Because if you are, then perhaps retirement isn't right for you. And that's okay.

I'm that type of person. I don't ever want to *fully* retire. "Fully" being the operative word here. But I digress. There'll be plenty more on that subject in Part 3 of the book.

For now, all I want you to do is take a little time to ask yourself, "Why do I want to retire?" and see what comes up. Ponder it for a while. There's no rush.

If nothing jumps to mind, then maybe that's because, as you're about to see in the next chapter, working actually does us a whole bunch of good.

CHAPTER 5

What We Get From Work

I KNOW, I KNOW, I know.

"But Gary," you're thinking, "Why in the world are you talking about work in a book about retirement? That's not what I'm here for, to talk about that thing I hate and can't wait to be rid of once and for all."

While it might be counterintuitive, talking *about* work in a book about quitting work is important. Because, as it turns out, in what is perhaps an ironic twist of fate, this thing you're so excited to ditch is actually good for you. Whether you realize it or not, work gives you a lot.

Money is the most obvious. There's a psychological component to earning. It makes us feel good. I know many people who take a great deal of satisfaction watching the numbers in their accounts go up. And, if you're like most people, your primary source of income comes from your job.

There are also social benefits. With the exception of a few occupations, most people have jobs that require them to be around people, whether co-workers, customers, or both. These interactions with others are meaningful.

Identity is something else you get from work, especially here in the Western world. There's a tendency for people to completely identify with their occupations. You can see it in the language we use when we talk about ourselves, "Hi, I'm Gary. I'm a financial advisor." We literally tell people we are what we do.

Finally, and maybe most importantly, work provides structure. It's the scaffolding around which many build their lives. This organizing principle of work is reinforced from an early age. How many times were you asked as a kid, "What do you want to be when you grow up?"

The thing is, structure, identity, social interaction, and feeling good about yourself are needs. It's not like they magically disappear when you retire. You still have to meet them. Only now the source you've been using to meet these needs is gone.

This is the big secret. This is how you retire and not die. Make sure all the needs you used to fulfill by working will be met when you stop. That's it. That's the trick. But, if you don't have a Plan for how you're going to accomplish that, it usually doesn't end well.

That's why I wrote this book. The chapters that follow give you the Tools you need to custom build a Plan tailored to your specific needs with the goal of creating a happy, successful, and long retirement. That's what we're doing here.

But, before we get to the Tools you'll use to build this Plan of yours, we need to make sure we get the foundation right. With that said, let's dig a little deeper into the needs I mentioned already, shall we?

STRUCTURE: YOUR SCAFFOLDING

Work, as I said, is an organizing principle. It's something your life has likely been built around. It's where you've spent most of your time. It's probably also been a focus of yours since you were a little kid.

For the first ten years of my life, whenever I was asked what I wanted to be when I grew up, my answer was, "Cowboy." Full stop. No hemming. No hawing. I wanted to be in the saddle and on the Plains.

Jokes aside, there's also something far more concrete you get from work: a schedule. Monday through Friday. Nine to five. Fifty weeks a year. You know where you are going to be, what you are going to do, and with whom.

This is a really big deal.

Since the time you were a child, you've had a schedule. And not only have you had one, but it's almost always been handed to you.

You go to school. This means catching the bus at a certain time, a time you didn't choose. You arrive. The bell rings. You sit down and do what you're told. Another bell rings. You get up and off you go to a new room. Or maybe you stayed put and switched subjects. At the end of the day, at the appointed time, it was back on a bus to go home. This was your routine. None of which you chose.

And then it's summer, your time of freedom and not being on a schedule. Except you probably were. I know I attended YMCA camp for two weeks and they kept us on a very tight schedule. Here for an hour. Over to the lake for the next. Across the way to the horses, where my childhood dreams of being a cowboy were crushed, and then to lunch at noon.

Eventually, summer ends. Back to school where the whole cycle repeats itself. This lasts for twelve years. Then maybe it's off to college or a tech school. Here you're given a bit more freedom. You get a say in what your schedule looks like, but there's still a schedule to follow.

Next stop, work. Where, once again, you find yourself handed another schedule to follow. One that presumably lasts for roughly forty-some years.

Your whole life has been scheduled. From the time you began toddling around to the time you retire, doing certain things at certain times is what you've always done. And rarely, if ever, have you created that schedule from scratch.

IDENTITY: WHO AM I?

"Your way of seeing the world bends around your work," writes Benjamin Percy in his book, *Thrill Me*. And he's right.

Because I'm a financial advisor, I spend the majority of my time talking to people about money. I see the world through the lens of money and numbers. I never made a conscious choice for it to be this way. It's not like I said to myself, "Gary—numbers. And math. That's the ticket. Those are the best ways to make sense of the world." It just happened.

If you're like most people, you introduce yourself and say, "Hi, My name's *so-and-so*. I'm a/an <*insert occupation*>. It's nice to meet you." You tell new people you meet you are what your job is. The interesting part is, most people don't even realize they do this.

Words and concepts aside, there's also an element of status at play here too. Many people look to work in order to feel Purpose. What they accomplish professionally makes them feel as though they've been using their time in a meaningful way.

I'LL SHOW YOU

One of my clients, Diane, came to see me. She was the top salesperson in her company and retired recently. When I saw her, she looked worn out and tired. This struck me as odd. Normally, Diane was always bouncing around the room, she had so much energy. Something was clearly out of sync.

"Hey, Diane. How's retirement?" I asked.

She exploded.

"It's awful. I hate it. In one week, one stinking week, I went from closing multi-million dollar sales and feeling important to lugging two cans out to the curb. I'm serious, Gary. The most important thing I did last week was take out the trash. I hate it."

I'd known Diane for over twenty years. She was always passionate about her job, loved her life, and knew who she was and what she was doing. Now, after a single week of retirement, she was lost.

SOCIAL CONNECTIONS

Don't underestimate the relationships you had at work. And I'm not talking about just the weekly or daily lunch dates with your favorite co-workers. The low-grade social interactions between you and your customers and the people you weren't especially close with mattered too.

Being around other people is extremely important. That doesn't go away when you retire. So, if retiring and not dying is your goal, then you need to meet this need. I'm serious. This is a mental health issue.

You need to be around other people. We all do. Isolation and loneliness are not parts of the happy, successful retirement formula. In fact, research suggests they're deadly, comparable to smoking fifteen cigarettes per day.

We are social animals, first and foremost. Your brain, just like mine, reflects this, There's a phenomenon called "limbic regulation" which basically says brains and nervous systems need to be around other brains and nervous systems in order to function well.

Limbic regulation is something you probably got from work.

DOLLARS AND SENSE

Life is hard. Not having enough money makes it harder. That's just how it is.

The fact is, you need a certain amount of money for the basic necessities of life. I'm talking about food, clothing, shelter, and water. Because no matter who you are, it's a lot harder to be in a good place mentally, physically, and emotionally if you're hungry, thirsty, cold, and homeless.

But money isn't the only thing that matters. There are people whose entire sense of self-worth is tied up in how much money they make. They tend to constantly compare themselves to everyone they meet. It's almost like somewhere along the line these people decided keeping score was important and that money was the way to do it. Simply put, their increase in net worth equated to "winning life."

I'm not in love with this form of measurement. Not that there's anything wrong with having ample funds. Earning and amassing a fortune is a great accomplishment, one to celebrate to be sure. It's the obsession that troubles me.

I'm amazed at how many retired people I meet that are still so focused on their net worth. It's like they are incapable of actually enjoying the fruits of all their years of labor. Instead, they're worried or stressed about how to keep growing their wealth.

Money is a tool. Like any other tool, it's only as good as what you use it for.

Having touched upon what we get from work, I'd like to take a moment to share a cautionary tale. Because let's be honest here, knowing what we're supposed to do is one thing. I know I'm supposed to eat more vegetables.

Actually doing it? That's a whole other enchilada. I hate kale.

WHEN NEEDS GO UNMET

One day my wife, Linda, and I were heading out of town. Instead of driving to the airport, I grabbed us a Lyft. The gentleman who picked us up was probably in his early seventies. Being the friendly and curious guy that I am, I struck up a conversation.

"So, how long have you been driving for Lyft?" I asked.

"You know, I retired from my sales job after forty years," he said, looking at me in the rearview mirror. "And I knew after a month if something didn't change, I was either going to kill myself, or my wife was going to do it for me."

All three of us laughed.

"I didn't know what to do with my time," he said. "I could only read so many Lee Child novels and I was getting depressed just sitting around. I'm a social guy. I've spent my entire life around people. As a salesman, I was used to spending my days calling, meeting, and talking. Being alone for so many hours was driving me crazy."

"That sounds tough," I said.

"I knew I had to get out of the house, right? Well, I decided becoming a 'mall-walker' would be a good idea. You know, get some exercise. Except, it turns out they sell stuff at those places. I found myself buying all sorts of things I didn't need. I don't even like to shop. I just wanted something to do to kill time...instead it ended up killing my bank account."

"It gets worse" he said. "Bear with me because I know this sounds crazy, but it's like I didn't know who I was anymore. For most of my life, whenever I met anyone, I'd say something like, 'Hey, I'm Leroy, I sell printers and copiers. It's nice to meet you.' But the first time I introduced myself to one of my fellow mall-walkers, I didn't know what to say. I was speechless. It's like when I quit my job, I lost a part of who I was."

At this point, I kind of regretted starting this conversation. And by the side-eye look Linda gave me, I knew she did too. However, we were still a ways away from the airport and I was already in too deep to not ask a follow-up question.

"So, that's when you became a Lyft driver?"

"This was my wife's idea," he said. "It's been great. I've always loved driving and talking. I'm not getting rich, but that was never what it was about for me. I just needed to get out of the house, be around people, and have something to do. Now, I'm loving retired life. I start working when I want to, usually around 9:30ish and drive until 1. Then I catch up with some buddies for a late lunch before heading home."

"I'm glad you found your rhythm," I said.

"Me too."

The rest of our ride passed uneventfully. We talked about Cleveland sports until we arrived at the airport. As Linda and I were waiting to check our bags, I made a note to include Leroy's story in the book.

INSIGHTS

Let's take a moment to appreciate all the things you get from work. It does a lot more for us than providing the food, clothing, and shelter we typically give it credit for. Those hours you spent at your chosen profession gave you structure, social interaction, identity, and money—all of which you still need to enjoy your retirement.

Leroy, our Lyft driver, was a great example of what happens when your main source of these needs goes away. He didn't have a clue how to meet these needs, and you saw what happened. This is why a Plan is one of the 3 Ps that will keep you young and help you have a healthy, happy retirement.

Let's do a quick recap of Part 1. You know how we got here. You've spent a little bit of time thinking about why you want to retire. You've learned that the trick to a happy retirement is to make sure your needs are being met.

Now, there's one last stop we need to make, one more crucial component that is foundational to your happy, healthy, and successful retirement before moving on to Part 2. It involves your mindset. Ready? Perfect.

CHAPTER 6

Your Retirement Mindset

ARE YOU RETIRING FROM something or to something? One of the most important and foundational aspects of a successful, happy retirement is getting your mind right. I say "right" for a reason, because there is definitely a healthy mindset you can have while heading into your retirement, and there's an unhealthy one. The healthy one helps you approach retirement in a positive way. The unhealthy one… well…use your imagination.

It's easy to view retirement as an ending. Who wouldn't? It's a milestone marking the end of a massive phase of your life, perhaps the longest. It's the end of your punching the clock and going to work.

Endings are closely tied to grief. This is because endings create space. They free us, whether or not we want it, from the way things used to be and that feels like a loss. Getting stuck in the endings and what's being "lost" are traits of the unhealthy retirement mindset.

We become so used to doing certain things at certain times, in certain places with certain people and then—BAM!—all this routine goes away. One day you've got all this structure, and the next, it's gone. This absence of structure typically triggers feelings of discomfort and uncertainty about the future.

My friend, Grace, described it best. She's a politician who had a remarkable string of successes. She went sixteen years without losing an election. Then, one day, her winning streak came to an end.

"I was in a state of disbelief and shock," she told me. "I lost. My term was going to end in two months and I didn't know what to do, let alone what to think."

The thing about discomfort is that most of us will do anything in our power to get away from the "dis" and get back into the comfort.

In the midst of discomfort, it's easy to look at the past. Ignoring the impact of all the things that made you crazy, you long for the comfort of what was. We're so drawn to this comfort and what's familiar, it's like we look back through rose-colored glasses.

Remember "Glory Days" by Bruce Springsteen? It's like that. So many people I've met sit around during their retirement reminiscing about how good it used to be, how good they had it, as they watch their lives pass them by.

Without question, this is not the retirement mindset you want. It's what Carol Dweck, in her book, *Mindset: The New Psychology of Success*, would call a fixed mindset. And it's one I call "wrong."

It's the exact opposite of the mindset you want. This fixed or wrong mindset is a way of looking at your situation and sabotaging yourself. It saps your energy and puts you on the path to an earlier grave.

That's not what you want. That's not what I want for you. That's not why you picked up this book. You're reading this because you want to have a long, successful retirement. And that, my friends, comes from having a growth mindset.

Because, as luck would have it, endings carry with them the seeds of new beginnings. You want to be here, focusing on the seeds, on the new beginnings. This is your growth mindset.

This is the beginning of your happy and healthy retirement. This is your first step. Instead of being stuck and fixated on what's been lost, you need to put your attention and energy into all you've gained by saying goodbye to work.

Here are a few strategies and suggestions to help you get out of the wrong retirement mindset and into the right one.

FROM ANTICIPATION TO ENJOYMENT

By far, the issue I notice the most is how uneasy my clients are early in their retirement. As I've previously touched on, not working comes with its fair share of mental and emotional challenges. One I haven't mentioned yet has to do with shifting from anticipation to enjoyment.

Retirement flips a long-held script you've lived by. Before retirement, you lived functionally. This means you provided for yourself and possibly your family. It also means you made choices in the present that were investments in the future.

But what happens when the future becomes the now, when the moment you've been waiting for and saving for arrives? Your new job becomes living that future, doing all the things you want to do and enjoying your time.

This is often easier said than done.

Up until now, your whole mindset has been one of investing, saving, and planning. Now, here you are. You made it. It's the future. It's the time you've been looking forward to. And it's also time to adopt a new mindset that more accurately fits your situation.

You've got to learn how to enjoy the present. You've got to stop looking at tomorrow and start enjoying today. Except, you've spent thirty plus years focusing on tomorrow.

Making this switch is going to take time. It's going to take practice. And that's okay. You're breaking an old habit that's been with you for a very long time. One this book is designed to help you with.

"TAKE THIS JOB AND SHOVE IT"

The truth is, how you felt when you left your job has a huge influence on what the next best step is for you.

If you're someone who's excited about retiring and beginning this next phase of your life, then you're well on your way to having the right retirement mindset. You've already framed retirement in a healthy way. It's likely you have a good idea of meaningful ways to fill your time and you're excited for this new phase.

However, there's another possibility. Maybe you left a toxic workplace. Maybe it took everything in your power just to show up and get through the day. Or perhaps you were forced out unexpectedly. Circumstances outside your control may have moved you into retiring before you wanted to, and now you're left feeling bitter and resentful.

If this is you, I have one word for you: Decompress.

I mean it.

Don't go charging into your retirement full speed ahead. As much as you may want to, because throwing yourself into the "next thing" is what you've always done, I'm telling you—don't.

Take a breather. Slow down. Rest. Recover.

You've got the time for that now. You're retired. Taking good care of yourself is something you need to do if you want to live a long time.

IF IT STILL HURTS

I had a client who really struggled with life after work. His story is one I want to share.

Martin spent his career as a union representative. He spent the first few months of his retirement moping around, feeling sorry for himself, and focusing on what he'd lost. Clearly, Martin wasn't doing himself any favors when it came to his mindset. Finally, after having had enough, he called his closest friends and invited them over for a cookout and bonfire. Little did his friends know what was in store for them.

Martin had just finished reading Marie Kondo's, *The Life-Changing Magic of Tidying Up: The Japanese Art of Decluttering and Organizing*. And, like many things in Martin's life, he decided to put his own spin on what he learned from her book.

After everyone ate and drank their fill and the fire was blazing, Martin disappeared without saying a word.

Moments later, his friends spotted him pushing what looked like a wheelbarrow overflowing with stuff. He parked next to the fire and turned to his friends.

"First, I want to thank you for coming. As you all know, I retired recently," he said to a chorus of cheers. "Now what some of you might not know is how hard it's been on me. But earlier this week I got an idea."

With that, Martin reached over to the wheelbarrow, pulled something off the top, and chucked it into the fire.

"Welcome" he said, smile beaming, "to my career's funeral."

The wheelbarrow he quietly hauled up to the fire was full of pictures, awards, knick-knacks, and mementos from his work life. He was burning them all as a way of saying goodbye and moving on.

Now I know what some of you are thinking. Yes. What Martin decided to do is definitely on the extreme side and possibly dangerous. And no. Marie Kondo does not demand you torch your past.

But Martin swears it's one of the best choices he's ever made. "Gary, I really think it was the turning point," he told me over lunch.

There's a reason almost every culture throughout history has some sort of ritual they perform for the dead. Funerals are for the living, not the dead. It's a way for us to honor the past, say goodbye, and move into the future.

In Martin's case, it wasn't a person he needed help saying goodbye to; it was his career. And if you find yourself in a similar place, do what Martin did. Throw yourself a work funeral.

I'm serious.

1. **Collect some knick knacks**—The stuff that used to be on your desk, your name tag, or anything from your work life.

2. **Make sure it's nothing you want to keep**—There ain't no turning back...

3. **Do what Martin did**—Invite your friends over and feed them. Then give your career a eulogy. Talk about the things you liked at work and those you didn't. There isn't a wrong way to eulogize your work. Just say the words you need to. Express your emotions and attachments. Let it flow. Say your proper goodbye.

4. **Let it go**—Then, once you've said all there is to say, wish everything you've gathered well, and throw it all away. Or, be like Martin, and burn the hell out of them in a beautiful blaze of glory. Then, as an added bonus, if you remember the marshmallows you get to have farewell s'mores too!

Like I said, it might sound a little weird and non-traditional, but that doens't mean it's not powerful. Honor what you're leaving behind. Let go of what's keeping you stuck. Bury the past and with it your unhealthy retirement mindset.

Create space. Embrace your future. Invite a newer, healthier mindset into your life. This is the first step on your path to a bigger, better, more beautiful life.

Having the right retirement mindset sets the stage for the healthy, happy, and successful retirement you want. Without it, you've got no chance. With it, you've got at least a fighting one.

The right mindset is one that realizes retiring is a marathon, not a sprint. It also recognizes that a healthy, happy, and successful retirement is something that is built over time. It doesn't automatically fall into your lap, nor is retirement something you should expect yourself to be automatically good at. If you're struggling, it doesn't mean you're a failure and doomed. It means you're normal and have to practice.

That's right. Practice. Be honest. How often have you picked up something in your life or tried something new, and were instantly a rockstar, or even above average at it?

That's not how life works for most people, and that's certainly not how retirement works for most people. So expect to struggle a bit. There'll be up days and down days.

All this means is you need to practice; you're not there yet.

And if you're really struggling, take a page out of Martin's book. Throw yourself a work funeral. It might be just the ticket.

Oh, in case you're wondering about my politician friend from earlier in the chapter, Grace took a year off to reassess her life after her defeat, jumped back in, and hasn't lost an election since.

Now, give yourself a pat on the back. You've just finished the last little bit of groundwork, and as You're about to learn in Part 2, that's certainly a Win worth celebrating.

PART 2

CHAPTER 7

Tools

WELCOME TO PART 2!
In Part 1, we talked about a few foundational things necessary to retire and not die. That groundwork is going to be the basis for what comes next, or the drumbeat, if you will, of your kickass retirement song.

Having learned about the history of retirement, why it's something we expect to do, everything you get from work, and the all-important retirement mindset, it's now time to turn toward building. And what do you need to have in order to build something? Tools.

This is what Part 2 is all about (if you couldn't tell from the title). Here you're going to be introduced to the exercises and concepts you'll use to build the retirement of your dreams. Some of the exercises ahead are a bit like a fine wine or a stew. The longer you sit with them and let them breathe or marinate, the better they taste.

But I'm getting ahead of myself. Before going any further, I'd like to tell you a story. It's one that touches on a handful of Tools we'll be talking about.

"CAT'S IN THE CRADLE"

I wouldn't call myself a huge Harry Chapin fan, but that song is one that has always struck me. Maybe it's because the best mentor I ever had was my dad. Throughout my career, he was there as an example, providing guidance and wisdom. I was fortunate enough to have a first-class seat to watch how my father handled his transition into retirement.

Dad loved Florida. And so did my mom. They bought a condo on a golf course in West Palm Beach. Sure, escaping Ohio winters was a big factor, as my mom hated those, but it wasn't the only one. It was the social life that sold them.

The golf course had a thriving membership. There was a beautiful clubhouse boasting tons of activities, a good restaurant, and an even better bar. Upon joining, my parents were treated to an instant social life.

This was huge, at least for my dad. My mom? The only thing she cared about was getting out of the cold. But dad had a Plan.

He was smart and made up his mind to split his time between Ohio and Florida. Dad saw plenty of his friends and clients make the mistake of diving in and moving to a new place when they retired only to regret it. He knew to test the waters before jumping in.

For the first couple of years, he alternated weeks. He'd go to Florida, spend time with my mom and his friends in the sun for a week, and then fly back to Ohio. Then, he'd spend the next week taking care of his clients and sporting a good tan, before heading down South again.

I vividly remember when he put "phase two" of his Plan into effect. It was in February, on one of those bitter nights where the wind whips and wallops your breath.

I was picking him up at the airport. After he got into the car and blew on his hands to warm them up, he said, "This is it. This is the sign I was waiting for."

Now, my father was not a mystical man. To hear him mention something about a message from the universe had me puzzled to say the least. "What do you mean, Dad?" I asked.

"I've been thinking about changing my routine. I knew it was something I wanted to do eventually. Now, I'm going to start spending two weeks in Florida and coming back here for one."

"Oh, okay," I said. "But what was the sign?"

He smiled and pointed at the temperature gauge. It was seven degrees.

Phase two lasted for two more years. This two week/one week split served him well. But toward the end of the second year, I could see the writing on the wall. One day, he popped into my office.

"Gary" he said, "I'm ready. I'm going to make the switch. I'm going to start spending the entire winter in West Palm."

"I think that's a great choice, Dad," I said. "What took you so long?"

At this point, he reached into his sport coat and pulled out his calendar book. It was the same one I'd seen him use and replace for thirty years. He handed it to me.

I remember flipping through and being amazed. Every day of every week for the next four months was chock full of activities. Golf, bridge, dinners, lunches, parties—every day was scheduled. I handed the book back.

"This is why I didn't want to move to Florida immediately," he said. "I needed to make sure there would be enough things to do down there. I know too many people who've made a move like this, got there, and then were bored to death. Their life revolved around drinking and hitting early bird specials, and I didn't want that to be me."

It was ironic that Dad's calendar, something he always pointed to as one of the keys to his success at work, was now a key to creating his successful retirement.

INSIGHTS

My dad shared two very crucial secrets with me about retirement. The first and most obvious was the need for a Plan, which, if you haven't noticed by now, is what this whole book is about. The second, more subtle secret, is to use some of the same tactics and strategies you applied to become successful at work to be successful at retirement. That's the next five chapters in a nutshell—using what worked at work.

Then, the final chapters of this section are about the other 2 Ps that will keep you young: Passion and Purpose. These are your more "advanced" Tools.

Think of the ideas and practices in these early chapters of Part 2 as your simple Tools; your screwdriver, wrenches, etc. The later ones? Those are your power Tools.

And by the time you finish Part 2, you'll have learned the importance of not reinventing the wheel, an easy scheduling method, and how to stay more motivated. You'll also pick up tips about how to feel better about yourself and your life, a few things about two of the Ps, and get a better sense of good ways to fill your time.

Sound good?

I think so too.

CHAPTER 8

Your Retirement Role Model

WHEN IT COMES TO using and applying the things we did at work to make us successful in retirement, I'd like to start with mentorship.

In my other books, *If Your Money Talked* and *The American Dream Revisited*, I wrote about mentors. And I always knew mentorship would make an appearance in this book too, especially since it's a great way to fill some retired free time. What I didn't see coming was this chapter.

But the more people I talked to about their retirement, the more it became apparent that mentorship wasn't just something that mattered throughout their career and then disappeared. It was something that mattered every bit as much in retirement. And probably not in the way you think.

I assumed the mentorship I'd be talking about in this book would focus on the positive aspects of *being* a mentor. But a fate-filled day of meetings with clients showed me the light…

IT STARTED LIKE ANY OTHER DAY

It was finally Spring and one of the first sunny days after a long, gray Ohio winter. The air was crisp and fresh, and I found myself smiling as I pulled into the parking lot at my office. I'm sure it was a combination of the weather and the fact one of my all-time favorite tunes, Talking Heads' "Burning Down The House," was on the radio.

I was in a good mood, excited to start my day.

My first appointment was with a client who'd been retired for over a decade. My second was a meeting with an executive who was about to retire. Then I was free for lunch before I had to make a late-afternoon presentation at a nearby company.

Jerry walked into the office at 9:45 sharp, sporting the same big smile I'd come to expect from him. He'd always been prompt and possessed a profound love of life. Both when he was working and after he retired. Jerry was also a planner, the type of guy who had his entire vacation scripted down to the minute, months before he packed a single bag.

It was a routine meeting. After being retired for a decade, Jerry wanted to make sure he was still good-to-go from a financial perspective. Like I've said, money is always the first thing people want to discuss. Jerry was no exception. So, we went over his accounts and I reassured him he was in great shape. Hearing this, his smile somehow grew bigger.

Seeing he was in a good mood, and since we wrapped up our meeting with time to spare, I decided to ask him the question I'd been asking all of my happily retired clients.

"*What's your secret?* So many people come into my office and sit in the exact chair you're sitting in and look miserable. But not you. You're the exception, Jerry. You are one of the happiest retired people I know, and it seems like you've been retired forever."

"Gary, it's been twelve years since I walked away from my job," he said. "But I never walked away from my life. The idea of having unlimited time to explore new interests keeps me going. I've tried my hand at quite a few things, some with great success, and others have been less than stellar."

"Seems logical," I said. "How do you find new things to do?"

"I'm lucky. My neighbor is retired too, and he invites me to tag along when he goes and does new things. We learned how to play golf, we've taken cooking classes, pottery classes, and even started to learn to play guitar in hopes of starting a band. He's like my retirement mentor."

I didn't have a ton of time to digest Jerry's answer because my next client, Kristen, was waiting. I thanked Jerry for his business and his time, and for sharing his secret.

With that, we said our goodbyes.

Enter, Kristen.

She and I have been working together for years. She recently turned 65 and was planning to retire. Like most everyone in her position, Kristen made an appointment to see me in order to make sure she had enough money. No surprise there. It's always the first topic.

"Congratulations, Kristen," I said. "You're set up to have a fine retirement, financially speaking. That's no small feat. That said, I've got to ask you my new favorite question."

"Of course, Gary," she said. "Shoot!"

"You've been working at your company for thirty-five years. That's a long time. What's next? What are you going to do with the rest of your life?"

"You know, Gary, it's funny. One of my friends retired a few years ago and she asked me the very same question. At the time, I hadn't thought about it at all. When I gave her my answer, she shook her head and said, 'Retirement ain't all it's cracked up to be. I spent the first three months depressed before I finally figured out what I was doing. Why don't you and I start spending more time together and I'll show you the ropes.'"

"That's incredible!" I said. "Have you taken her up on her offer?"

"Absolutely. And it's been great. She's totally taken me under her wing and showed me what it takes to have a happy retirement."

"What's that look like?" I asked.

"It's perfect. We get together a couple times a week and go do things. Last week, we volunteered together as ticket takers for a fundraiser. If the weather's nice, we spend time outside. If it's not, we go to a museum or a movie. We schedule two daytime and two nighttime activities each week. She's taught me so much."

"Like what?"

"For the past few months, every time we sit down for a bite to eat or something to drink, she tells me about an issue she's had to face in her retirement, how she struggled with it, the mistakes she made, and what ended up working for her. She's my retirement mentor."

"Kristen, that has got to be one of the smartest retirement strategies I've heard. And these days it seems like all I do is talk to people about retirement," I joked.

My next appointment was a twenty-minute drive away. The whole time in the car I was thinking to myself, a retirement role model. How cool is that? I can't believe I hadn't thought of that. What a great idea...

The drive flew by. And it wasn't because I was speeding. Well, maybe a little.

Plus, my good music karma kept rolling. About ten minutes into the drive, my favorite radio station, 91.3, The Summit, started one of their Beatles Breaks. As soon as I heard the first notes of "Baby You Can Drive My Car" I rolled down the windows and started singing. The building guitar intro of "Get Back" followed immediately on its heels. So, I kept the windows down, kept singing, managed not to get pulled over for speeding or disturbing the peace, and before I knew it, I was where I needed to be.

I walked in and handed my card to the gentleman behind the desk. "I'm Gary Sirak. Here to see Barbara."

"Welcome, Mr. Sirak. Barbara will be with you shortly," he said. "Why don't you take a seat and I'll let you know when she's ready for you?"

Just then, I heard my name. Looking up, it was my friend James, who also worked at this company. "I was just thinking about you," he said. "You got a second to talk? I'd love to bounce some ideas off you."

Catching up with James sounded way better than

pretending to look at old magazines, so I said, "Sure," and followed him into an empty conference room.

"What's up, James?"

"Well, it's getting to be about that time. I retire in a year and a half and wanted to set up an appointment to come see you to make sure I'm in good shape."

"Of course," I said. "I'd love to go over that with you. Call the office. Set up a time. Out of curiosity, have you put any thought into what you're going to do when you retire, or how you're going to spend the rest of your life?"

There was a pause. It became apparent that James, like so many others, didn't know how to answer this question. After a second or two, he responded.

"I...I didn't know. I've been so wrapped up in getting there that I've spent zero time thinking about what I'm going to do once I'm there. I guess I'm at a loss. I honestly don't know how I'm going to spend the rest of my life."

"Let me ask you another question, James. How many people do you know who've retired from this company?"

"Tons," he said.

"Have you ever considered reaching out to one of them and asking them how they spend their time?" I asked.

"No," he replied.

"Pick the happiest retired person you know and give them a call," I said. "Invite them to lunch or to get a cup of coffee and ask them their secret."

"That's a good idea. I'd never thought about that," said James, " but it makes so much sense. I know a bunch of people who're retired. I'll have to think for a bit about who the happiest ones are..."

"Whoever they are, I bet they'd be delighted to share what they've learned," I said. "There's no reason you have to figure this out all by yourself. You're not the first person to retire."

"Wow, Gary. I am so glad I ran into you today. What were the chances? Thank you so much," he beamed.

"My pleasure, James," I said as I turned to leave, "find a Retirement Role Model. It'll save you a lot of trouble."

A GOOD RETIREMENT ROLE MODEL IS...

Someone you know, like, and respect that you're comfortable sitting down with and asking questions.

Go find someone who's been where you're headed, done what you're trying to do, and succeeded. Learn from them. They are an incredible resource who can share pointers and prevent you from wasting your precious time.

WHY FINDING ONE MATTERS

I've watched too many clients, people I've cared about and worked with for years retire and fade away. And it always seems to start so innocently, so simply. All they want to do is take some time to relax. But then this period of relaxation goes on and on and on until they've been doing nothing for months.

Zilch. Zippo. Nada. They just sit around, watching tv. They stop moving. They stop doing things. And, before long, they stop living. In walking away from their job, they unintentionally end up walking away from their life.

Think about how many people you have watched go through this. My theory is these people had bad Retirement Role Models. At some point in their lives, they watched someone else retire this way and ended up following the same script and getting the same result.

FINDING A RETIREMENT ROLE MODEL

1. **Look around your life**—There's a good chance there's someone who fits the bill. It could be a relative, a good friend, a co-worker you admired, or an acquaintance from an organization you belong to.

2. **Reach out**—Once you have figured out who this person is, call them. Send an email or text.

3. **Say this**—"Hey, it's [*insert name*]—I'm trying to figure out how to retire and not die and you're the happiest retired person I know. How would you feel about letting me buy you a cup of coffee or take you to lunch to learn some of your secrets?"

I've found that most people are more than happy to share what they know and appreciate the opportunity to help someone who's genuinely interested. Especially if you buy them lunch.

Good Retirement Role Models are out there, waiting to be found. Just keep your eyes open and don't be afraid to strike up a conversation.

INSIGHTS

I have always believed that having role models—people who've done what you want to do and gone where you want to go—is important to success.

One of the major themes of Part 2 is that success is success. There's no reason to reinvent the wheel. You were successful enough to be able to retire. Why not use the things that helped you climb the mountain help you to live your marathon?

This means finding a mentor.

Think back to when you started your career. Did someone take you under their wing and show you the ins and outs? Didn't that help? Well, retirement is no different.

Chances are you know someone who's been successfully retired for a while. Pick up the phone and give them a call. See if they'd be willing to talk about how they've done it.

Take it from Jerry and Kristen. Follow the advice I gave James. Get yourself a Retirement Role Model.

Think of this person as the first Tool in your How-To-Retire-And-Not-Die Tool Box.

CHAPTER 9

3 Steps

I N FITTING WITH THE theme of Part 2, applying the same skills we used to become successful in our jobs to become successful in retirement, I'd like to tell you another story about the early days of my career.

When I was starting out as a life insurance agent, staying busy was my main goal. Well, that and making enough money to pay my mortgage and not starve. I quickly learned this meant I needed to do some serious planning on my part. Because it turns out people don't just appear and knock on your door asking to buy life insurance. Who knew?

After trying (and failing) with a number of different scheduling techniques, I decided to make up my own. I settled on three steps a day. That's how I decided to tackle advancing my career. My 3 Steps didn't always have to be something major like closing a sale or meeting with a prospective client. They just had to be actions that moved my needle toward success.

I'd design my day so I could take my first Step in the morning. Usually, it was something like having coffee or breakfast with a client, or a person I soon hoped might become one. My second Step, taken some time around lunch, would be a meeting with my mentor (otherwise known as my father), learning about a new product, or knocking out some paperwork. Finally, making cold calls during the afternoon was my go-to third Step. And as long as I took my Steps each day, doing three things aimed at success, I could go home happy and rest easy knowing it was a good day.

3 Steps is about accountability and incremental progress. I had it on good authority from my mentor that accountability and incremental progress were the keys to success in the insurance business. Consistent steps led to more sales. More sales led to more confidence. More confidence led to more sales.

Now, you ask, "What does advice about being successful selling insurance have to do with retiring?" The answer, it turns out, is a lot.

While the thought of waking up when you want to and not having anywhere to go sounds amazing at first, it doesn't age well. Having no schedule and nothing meaningful to do sneaks up on you fast.

If not properly prepared and planned for, retirement becomes empty. That's why I'm introducing you to my personal scheduling system, 3 Steps, that's guaranteed (hey—it worked for me!) to help you avoid the emptiness. And the best part? It's unbelievably easy to use.

Filling every minute of every hour of every day? No way. That's too much.

All you have to schedule are three different activities each day. That's it.

Start small. Remember—retirement isn't a 100-yard dash. It's a marathon.

As for the types of activities you should choose for your Steps, it depends. The short answer is to choose whatever you want. Just make sure you choose activities that are meaningful and that you enjoy. And if it's a longer answer you're after, keep reading. Part 3 goes into much more depth about this very topic.

Here's an example of the 3 Steps in action.

LAST WEEK

Wednesday I met my friend Shari for lunch. Her husband passed away a few months ago and I wanted to catch up with her. "How are you holding up?" I asked.

"Oh, Gary," she said. "Not a day goes by I don't miss him. Tom and I were married for over forty years. But you know what? One of the things you suggested after he passed helped me."

"Really?" Now, between you and me, I didn't have a clue what she was talking about. I say a lot of things.

She laughed. "I bet you don't even remember the conversation, but I sure do. I was feeling lost. I didn't know what to do or how to fill my time. I was overwhelmed and paralyzed in my confusion. That's when you told me about your 3 Steps."

"I did? Wow. I don't recall that at all," I said.

"It took me a while to be able to think straight, but when I finally could, I went right back to what you said. I started thinking about all the activities I enjoyed, all the things I could do, all the meaningful ways I could fill my time."

"I immediately thought of my grandchildren. I have three of them and they're all involved in sports. I used to love watching them, but when Tom got sick I stopped going to their games."

"Then, I realized how much I missed seeing them play. It was so much fun to cheer, socialize, and be around other people. Plus, the grandkids loved it. So, I decided to make going to their games one of my Steps. Now, I'm 'grandma in the stands' five nights a week. That means on those days I only need to figure out two other things to do, which is easy."

"That's wonderful, Shari. I'm glad I was able help."

"You and me both," she said. "I was so overwhelmed with...well...everything, but you gave me a way to structure my time that I could wrap my head around and use."

INSIGHTS

If my 3 Steps are good enough to help a grieving widow, I'm guessing they're good enough to help you too. Big transitions and changes in life almost always come with feelings of confusion and loss. It's not only natural but to be expected.

And in those times, keeping things simple is important. It's all too easy to get lost in thoughts of, "Now what?" or "What am I going to do with the rest of my life?" Coming back to what's here and now, focusing on doing three things today can serve to ground you and help keep those overwhelming thoughts at bay.

That's why I'm such a fan of this approach to scheduling. Well, that, and because it's mine, it works, it's easy, and it's one of the reasons I've had a very successful career as a financial advisor.

3 Steps.

That's the scaffolding we're going to use to support your retirement Plan. And now that you're familiar with it, let's move on and get acquainted with one of the main Tools you'll use for the actual building of your Plan.

CHAPTER 10

Welcome To Your WishList

TEN YEARS AGO, I was introduced to the "WishList" I had just started a course with Rex Houze's Better Performance & Results Inc., a company specializing in improving business performance. My coach, Don Harbert, gave me an exercise to complete.

"Gary," he said, "I want you to write down everything you hope to accomplish in this life. Dream big. Dream crazy. Use your imagination. Don't censor yourself. Let go. Have fun with this."

Now, it's not like the idea of creating a list of things you wish to do in your life is new. There was a feature film starring Morgan Freeman and Jack Nicholson made in 2007, *The Bucket List,* about this very thing. The two main characters put together a list of all the things they wanted to do before they died, and then went about doing them until...well... you can probably guess what happened.

While technically a "bucket list" and a "wish list" are the same thing, I think there's a big difference between them. That difference is perspective. The way you frame something matters. So does the language you use when you talk about it.

A bucket list focuses on getting things done before you die. There's a fearful pessimism along with a sense of fleeting time that colors a "bucket list." Not exactly uplifting, if you ask me.

A wish list is a whole different ball game. It's hopeful. It's optimistic. It affirms life. It's a collection of all the things you want to experience. And since you're reading a book about how to retire and not die, WishList it is.

I can't even begin to tell you all the positive vibes having a WishList has given my psyche. Every time I pull it out and look at it, I get excited. It's a reminder of all the things I want to do. Starting a WishList is both rewarding and important. It's one of the main Tools you'll use again and again to help you build your Plan in Part 3.

Follow the steps below. Take your time. Create your WishList. Get to know this Tool. You're going to need it later.

MAKING YOUR WISHLIST

1. **Go somewhere relaxing**—It could be a coffee shop, a restaurant, a bar, a patio, your favorite chair at home, a park, a bench, wherever. The idea is to put yourself in a physical environment you feel good in. You'll be doing some thinking and writing, so keep that in mind when choosing your spot. Some people prefer the energy of a busy place to help them get their juices flowing. Others prefer peace and quiet. Whichever you prefer, work with your natural inclinations. This will hereby be known as your "Thinking Place."

2. **Airplane mode**—This exercise shouldn't take long. The chances of a life-changing emergency that can't wait for the fifteen minutes it will take you to finish are slim. Turn your phone off. Or, at the very least, put it in airplane mode. Seriously. Do it.

3. **Relax**—There's no right or wrong way to relax. For me, I like to put on some music (usually David Bowie or the Beatles), pour myself a glass of wine, or make a mocha. Maybe you're a Heavy Metal and beer kind of person. Don't get bogged down in the details. Like the Isley Brothers sang, "It's Your Thing."

4. **Have supplies handy**—This book, something to write with, and something to write on will do the trick. I use a sheet of paper and draw a line down the center of it. Again, this is something you'll be referring back to often. A tiny scrap of paper or a napkin ain't gonna cut it.

5. **Ask yourself**—
What have I always wanted to achieve but never had the time for because I was too busy working?
Where have I always wanted to go?
What have I always wanted to see?
What have I always liked doing and wished I could do more of?
What have I always wanted to learn?

6. **Write down your answers**—DO NOT CENSOR YOURSELF. Let your imagination run wild. Ignore any self-conscious feelings. There isn't another person on the planet who'll see your WishList unless you choose to share it. In the words of Steve Winwood, "Roll With It." See what happens.

That's how you make your WishList.

Usually, one of two responses follow after talking to people about making their list. It's either wide-eyed excitement or a vacant stare. If you're the type of person who just had a million things flash into your mind, fantastic. Have at it.

If your palms are sweating, you've gone a little numb, and/or your mind is drawing a total blank—don't panic. I've included my own Wishlist at the end of this chapter as an example.

INSIGHTS

Your WishList is a living document. It's an ever-evolving work-in-progress, not written on stone tablets delivered on high from Mt. Sinai.

You don't have to finish it in a single sitting, but I can't emphasize enough how important it is to have a WishList moving forward. We'll be using this Tool a lot.

If, for whatever reason, you just aren't feeling it once you sit down, give yourself a break, and try again later.

Don't be surprised if, after you make your WishList, more things start randomly popping up. When they do, add them. I bet at least 50 percent of my ideas came to me while I was in the shower, driving, or listening to music.

Lastly, I'm going to repeat the same advice Don Harbert gave me:

"Dream big. Dream crazy. Use your imagination. Don't censor yourself. Let go. And have fun with this."

My Wishlist

- Take a basic technology course

- Start or join a book club

- Mentor a new financial advisor

- Visit all fifty States (forty down so far!)

- Attend Extraordinary Golf in Carmel, CA with Linda

- Travel to Sedona, AZ, Charleston, SC, Austin, TX, Savannah, GA, Napa Valley, CA

- Take a music cruise

- Write a best-selling book

- Go on a book tour

- Play forty rounds of golf a year

- Take a train across the Canadian Rockies

- Return to London and Paris

- Learn to play the bongos (only when Linda is outside)

- Write a song

- Cruise around on a private yacht

- Golf at Bandon Dunes and Pinehurst with Linda

- Spend more time in the Pacific Northwest

- Be a keynote speaker

- Help teach financial principles to youth

- Have a gallery show of my paintings (which reminds me...)

- Start painting again

- Cruise the Italian coast

- Attend a writer's conference

- Watch Cleveland play in all the Major League Baseball stadiums (six down)

- Tour the Canadian Capitals

- Write a book of spiritual stories

- Take a riverboat down the Mississippi and the Rhine

- Buy a home in Chautauqua, NY

- Visit more National Parks out West

CHAPTER 11

Your Retirement Key

H OW'D IT GO WITH your WishList?
Hopefully, really well and a whole bunch of fun...
The next Tool I'd like to introduce you to is your
Retirement Key. It's a "trick" to help you rethink retirement from my good friend and coach, Dan Sullivan. Much
like the WishList, the Retirement Key is simple in concept
and powerful in practice.

I first learned about it while attending Strategic Coach, a
program I've been attending for the past fifteen years. "The
trick," said Dan, "is to retire from everything you don't like
doing, and continue to do the activities you love and want to
do more of." Like I said, simple yet powerful.

Let's make yours. It's easy. I'll walk you through how to do it.

MAKING YOUR RETIREMENT KEY
Creating your Retirement Key is a lot like creating your
WishList.

1. **Gather your supplies**—Nothing too crazy is needed for
   this one. Just a piece of paper, something to write
   with, and a timer (which you have on your phone).

2. **Go to your Thinking Place**—Go back to the same setting you used to make your WishList. Or try somewhere else if that place doesn't work well for you.

3. **Airplane mode**—Yep. You guessed it, put the ol'digital "Do Not Disturb" sign on your phone.

4. **Relax**—Whatever this means to you, or in the words of my yoga teacher, "Breathe, Gary!"

5. **Get ready**—Divide your piece of paper into three columns. Label them Hates, Likes, and Loves. Set your timer for three minutes.

6. **Your Hates**—Start your timer. Write down every single thing you hate spending your time doing. Doesn't matter how big or how small. Nothing is off-limits. People. Places. Things. The funky smell coming from your basement. Anything goes.

7. **Your Likes**—Reset your timer for another three minutes. Now, list things you don't mind doing, that are so-so. Things that aren't as annoying as going to renew your driver's license, but not quite as delightful as "free fajita Fridays." Start the timer. Write all you can. Stop when it's time.

8. **Your Loves**—By now you know the drill. This time it's all about love. I want you to list the things you

absolutely, positively adore doing. I'm talking about the things you do that fill your cup, soothe your soul, and give you life. These are the loves we're looking for.

Congratulations! You've just constructed another Tool. There, that wasn't so bad? Was it?

On the off chance you struggled, I have included my own Retirement Key at the end of this chapter. Please use it as a reference point.

A word of caution: *Your* lists are the ones that matter. The Retirement Key only works if you're honest with yourself.

INSIGHTS

Once you've created your Retirement Key, share it with a few people who know you well. Choose folks from both your professional and personal life. They might help you fill in any gaps.

Overlooking things you love and/or are good at can be easy. When something is so second nature to you and comes naturally, sometimes you don't even notice it anymore. This is where the people who know you best come in. They can point out these blind spots.

I know because it happened to me.

It wasn't until I spoke to my good friend, Barry, and shared my Retirement Key with him that I became aware of a huge Love missing from my list.

"Yeah," said Barry. "I'd say you nailed it for the most part, Gary, but there's one thing you missed. There's nothing on here about connecting people. You're one of the best connectors I've ever met. You love bringing people together to solve problems."

I was floored. He was right. My love of "Connecting people" was so central to me, so natural and automatic, I blew right past it.

So, take it from me, share your Retirement Key with the people who know you best. They may think of something you didn't.

My Retirement Key

HATES

- Building things
- Trying to fix things (My handyman skills begin and end with changing a light bulb)
- Technology
- Paying bills
- Hitting the gym
- Onions
- Being cold
- Throwing things away

(What if I need my college term-paper on Outlaws of the Old West?!)

- Making a mess
- People who keep making the same mistakes
- People who aren't accountable
- Entitlement
- Losing
- Booking travel

LIKES

- Looking at Linda's garden (there's a very strict "no-touching" policy…)

- Washing my car

- Learning to play bongos

- Going to Rotary meetings

- Watching movies

- Playing golf

- Butter

- Meeting new people

- Being on the board of directors for organizations based on the arts and philanthropy

- Going to grocery stores

- Going to Farmers Markets

- Old-fashioneds

- Building teams

- Painting

- Writing books

LOVES

- Connecting people

- Reading Lee Child's Jack Reacher novels

- Crossing things off lists

- Traveling

- Music (David Bowie, The Beatles, Talking Heads, etc.)

- Ice cream

- Visiting Max in Colorado

- My WishList

- Good rye bread

- Matzo ball soup

- Breakfasts, lunches, and dinners at my favorite restaurants

- Mochas

- Helping others

- Sharing what I've learned

- Promoting my books

- Alternative healing modalities

- Long walks with my wife and son

- Being a mentor

- Meeting with my mentors

- Studying leadership

- Staying in touch with friends

- Cleveland sports

- Baseball

- Being in Chautauqua, NY

- Meeting friends for coffee

- Seeing plays

- Going to concerts

- Solving problems

CHAPTER 12

The Safety Talk

THIS DELIGHTFUL CHAPTER IS about regret, mistakes, and the ravages of time. Neat, huh?

You're welcome!

Here's how not to use the Tools we've talked about so far.

RALPH RUNS OFF

Meet Ralph. He and I had worked together for about fifteen years. As most of my clients do when it is time to retire, he scheduled an appointment to come see me.

"What can I do for you today, Ralph?" I asked.

"The first thing you can do is get up and get over here," he replied. Ralph was a hugger. "If it weren't for you, I'm not sure I'd have ever gotten to this point in my life. I'm a week away from cashing my last paycheck and retiring. I've been so excited, I've barely slept all week."

I smiled. "Just doing my job, Ralph. But it wasn't me. You deserve most of the credit. Getting advice is one thing. Actually listening to it and doing something? That's a whole other ballgame. Tell me, Ralph. What are you so excited about that's keeping you up at night?"

"I'm moving, Gary," he said. "I'm heading to San Diego. That's where my kids and grandkids are. That's where I want to be. There's so much to do there and the weather's great. I'll take the grandkids to the zoo, catch their baseball games, and go to the beach. But the thing I look forward to the most are the family dinners. I can't wait."

There was a little paperwork for Ralph to finish up and sign. Once all the "i"s were dotted and the "t"s were crossed, I wished him well on his big move.

"Thanks," he said. "I know it will be great. Take care of yourself, Gary. I'm not sure when I'll see you again, but I have your number so you'll be hearing from me. Next time I see you, I'll buy you dinner."

We hugged again and parted ways. As Ralph left, I remember thinking to myself, "There's a guy who's got it figured out."

Which is why I was completely stunned to see him walk into my office seven weeks later.

"Hey, Ralph," I said, a combination of surprised and confused. "What are you doing here? I thought it was all San Diego, sand, and sun from here on out."

"Gary," he said, "I screwed up. I don't know what I was thinking. San Diego is crazy. I never lived in such a busy, crowded place before. There were so many things I didn't even think about before I moved."

"Like what?" I asked.

"First off, remember how I told you how excited I was to spend more time with my family? Well, it turns out they have their own lives. Every time we got together, I felt like I was an outsider, in the way. Since they were the only people I knew out there, it didn't take long before I got lonely and started to miss Canton."

"And don't get me started on the traffic. It never stops. Never. It was crazy. I think I might have broken the record for being sworn at."

"What are you going to do now?" I asked.

"I'm moving back. I'm comfortable here. I have friends here and people who want to spend time with me. An occasional trip to visit my kids and grandkids is good enough. I don't have to live there."

"I'm sorry to hear your retirement didn't pan out the way you wanted, Ralph."

"Me too, Gary."

"So...you still buying me dinner?"

Ralph shook his head and laughed. "No way. Do you have any idea how much it costs to move across the country and back?"

ROADTRIPPING WITH RANDY AND SARAH

Randy and Sarah retired recently. When they were younger, they loved to go camping. They'd always talk about spending time outside, cooking over an open fire, sleeping under the stars, and a whole host of other fond memories of the great outdoors.

And for years, whenever either one of them had a stressful day at work, the other would always respond with something like, "Hang in there, hon. Before you know it, it'll be you and me in our new RV."

The number one thing on both of their WishLists was a cross country camping trip in an RV.

So, when they retired, naturally their first order of business was to buy an RV. They wasted no time. Since they'd been dreaming and talking about this trip for years, they had a route mapped out. They were going to cruise around the country visiting National Parks and anywhere else that piqued their interest.

It was going to be a three-month trip. First, they'd head south, avoiding the last remnants of winter. Then, they'd circle west before finally heading back north and east.

To say they were amped would be an understatement. Unfortunately, sometimes the best laid plans don't live up to expectations. One month into their trip, I got a call from Randy.

"How are the great outdoors?" I asked.

"Gary, this is probably one of the worst ideas I've ever had. And I've had a lot of 'em. It's been miserable," he said.

I could tell by his tone he wasn't kidding. "What went wrong?" I asked.

"What didn't? It took me a good week to even get comfortable behind the wheel of this thing. It's a far cry from my Toyota. This thing is like a Greyhound bus. Sarah totally refused to drive after five minutes behind the wheel, so I've done all the driving. Remember how we told you we had our whole trip mapped out, including places to stay?"

"Sure," I said.

"Yeah, well, it turns out we had a mechanical problem during the first week. Our whole schedule was thrown off.

Sarah spent an entire day calling National Parks trying to change our reservations. But the parks are crazy this time of the year. Most of them were booked solid. Our only option was to cancel."

"That's rough," I said.

"Oh, but wait, there's more. Let me ask you a question, Gary. When's the last time you slept in a tent?"

I thought about it for a second and flashed back to my time in the Tetons. "I bet it's been fifty years."

"Take it from me. Don't. Unless of course you want a painful reminder of how damn old you are. Sarah and I did it once. I couldn't walk for three days."

Randy was on a roll.

"Sarah and I are on our way back to Canton. We should be there in a couple of days. Let's the four of us grab dinner. We have some pretty funny stories for you and Linda."

"I look forward to it," I said. "Let me know when you're back."

"Will do. Hey, Gary, real quick before I let you go…you don't happen to know anyone looking to buy a slightly used RV, do you?"

INSIGHTS

My hope is that by pointing out how Ralph, Randy, and Sarah misused their Tools, you won't make the same mistakes and misuse yours.

Let's start with Ralph. His story illustrates two really important points. One has to do with your dreams of spending time with other people, family included. The other is about packing up your life and moving to a new place. Either of which could be on your WishList and Retirement Key:

"I'm going to spend more time with <blank>."

"I'm moving to <blank>."

If anything remotely resembling the first item appears on your WishList, then great. Spending time with the people who are important to you is a fine choice. However, do the people you're planning to spend more time with know your plans? Because not everyone may be as excited about the proposition as you are.

Like Ralph learned, other people have their own lives. They already have friends to see, places to go, things to do, and none of those may include you. It might be harsh, but as in Ralph's case, it might also be true.

So, if *"spending more time with <blank>"* appears anywhere on your WishList or Retirement Key, PLEASE TELL THEM. Make sure everyone is on the same page, especially before you pick up and relocate.

Which brings me to lesson two from Ralph…

Hey, look. I get it. I've spent my entire life in Northeast Ohio. I know all about long winters and gray skies. I understand the allure of always being able to see the sun.

But, before you move, here's a short list of questions to consider:

How much time have you spent there?

Do you know anyone there?

Have you visited this place at different times throughout the year?

Have you experienced all four seasons there?

Sometimes, dreams need to be challenged in order to see if they measure up. I beg you to think through and expose yourself to some of the real-world, logistical, day-to-day issues of moving to a new place. The best way you can do this is by visiting at different times throughout the year.

When you're there, strike up a conversation with a long-time local or two. Ask them what their favorite and least favorite times of year are and why. Chances are, their answers may surprise you.

I can't even count how many clients I've had who've bought a place, packed up their lives, and moved, only to end up regretting it. It's one reason I'm a big fan of the adage, "Try before you buy." Which, incidentally, brings us back to Randy and Sarah.

The biggest takeaway from their story is, if something like, *"I'm going to spend more time doing <blank>,"* is in the works as a potential part of your Plan, try before you buy.

Sarah and Randy could have easily rented an RV for a weeklong trip to see how it went. Instead, they jumped in head-first, and wouldn't you know it? "Life on the road" turned out to be better in their imaginations than it actually was on the road.

My advice? Dunk a toe. Don't dive in. The water might be freezing and not as pleasant as you imagined.

Ask yourself:

Is there a small, first step I can take? Figure that out. Take it. That way you can learn...

Do I still enjoy <blank>?

We all have a tendency to look back fondly and remember how much we used to enjoy certain things. Notice the words "used to." Because, and I hate to break this to you, YOU AREN'T 20 OR 30 OR 40 ANYMORE.

I know I told you to think back and tap into the things you used to like to do for your WishList. I stand by that. But here's the thing...

The past is tricky. Living in it is a mistake. After *thinking* back, you need to come back. To reality. To who you are and where you are today.

People change. Minds change. Bodies change. What we like changes. What hurts changes.

Look, when I was younger I loved playing basketball. It was my absolute favorite thing to do. Today? It would be a total disaster. I'd get injured just looking at the ball, let alone stepping onto the court.

That's just how it is. Accepting the truth, adapting to what is, and being flexible beats the hell out of the alternatives.

Fighting reality, denying the truth, and torturing yourself are *not* how to live your marathon.

Okay. Thus concludes our safety talk. See? That wasn't so bad. Now, please remove your industrial strength safety glasses, deposit them in the bin by the door, and move along to the next chapter.

CHAPTER 13

Celebrating Wins

THIS NEXT TOOL IS a little bit like a battery pack. It serves to super-charge all the others, making them more effortless to use, and leaving you more energized and feeling better about yourself.

Stick with me because I'm about to let you in on a big secret. Do you want to know what else helps you have a good retirement? Feeling good about yourself and your life.

That's what this chapter and Tool are all about—increasing the good energy you feel. Because, and correct me if I'm wrong here, you didn't work your whole life so you could retire and feel like crap, did you?

Right now the thrill of never having to go to work again may be enough. This is especially true of the newly retired. But the truth is, being newly retired is a lot like being newly married. The honeymoon, with all its excitement and joy, will end.

Which is why this chapter is so very important.

The best way I've found to keep myself motivated and engaged throughout my professional and personal life is by setting goals and rewarding myself when I achieve them. Or, to put it another way, "getting wins" and celebrating them.

It goes like this...

Set goal. Achieve goal. Celebrate Win. That's the system. That's the formula.

So, easy in concept, trickier in practice. Many people have a tendency to rush onto the next goal before taking the time to truly stop, appreciate it, congratulate themselves, and celebrate what they just accomplished.

And when it comes to goal setting, most people set their sights on work. It's in the office or on the job where we tend to reach for specific accomplishments. But since you're retired, or thinking about it, that's not going to fly.

Once you're no longer working, there are no more sales goals or quarterly reports you can use to tap into the feel-good magic of getting and celebrating Wins. This means it's time to get creative. You'll need to redefine your Wins, figure out how you're going to achieve them, and most importantly, how you're going to celebrate them.

Below are examples of some new types of Wins for your new type of life.

POTENTIAL RETIREMENT WINS

- Crossing something off your WishList.

- Spending time on a Love from your Retirement Key.

- Tackling a necessary evil (like "Paying bills") from your Hates.

- Taking your 3 Steps for the day.

- Going to your favorite restaurant.

- Exercising.

- Spending time outside in nature.

- Seeing your friends.

- Seeing your family.

- Not getting into a fight with your family.

- Eating your vegetables for the day.

You get the point.

CELEBRATING YOUR WINS

Fortunately, the way you celebrate your Wins doesn't necessarily have to change now that you're no longer working. And for the record, you don't have to do anything lavish or fancy. Just look at the list below:

My Favorite Ways to Celebrate

- Drinking a hot fudge milkshake or a mocha.

- Meeting my friends for dinner.

- Going for a long walk.

- Attending concerts.

- Putting on a new pair of socks. (I'm serious. New sock days are some of my favorite days...).

- If I'm traveling, getting my shoes shined.

These are some of the day-to-day ways I celebrate my Wins. But going on a vacation or drinking a nice bottle of wine work too, if that's more your speed.

How you celebrate doesn't matter nearly as much as *that* you celebrate.

If you're still a little unclear about what getting and celebrating Wins looks like, here's an example from my own life...

LAST TUESDAY

I met a friend for coffee. This was my morning Step. He was struggling with some business stuff so I listened and offered advice. This counts as a double Win. Not only did I have something scheduled for my morning (one of my 3 Steps), but I also got to help someone with their problems (one of my Loves).

In celebration of my two-Win morning, I treated myself to a peppermint mocha.

Later that afternoon, I attended a Rotary meeting (another Win since the meeting was my afternoon Step). By sheer chance, I ended up sitting next to a gentleman I'd known casually. As the meeting was wrapping up, he turned to me.

"Any chance you've got a few minutes after the meeting to chat?" he asked. "There are a couple of things I'd like to run by you."

"Sure," I said. So, I stuck around for maybe twenty

minutes and answered questions about Social Security. This was another Win, as I got to do that same Love again, helping someone solve their problems.

I was amped. I was up four Wins for the day and feeling pretty good about myself (I guess it could have been the mocha…) Anyway, my next stop was home. And because I was feeling so good and had all this energy, I decided to tackle one of my Hates, "Paying bills."

Now, I know what you might be thinking, but hear me out. I hate "Paying bills." Not for the obvious reason of spending hard-earned cash, but because it means I have to use the computer.

If you go back and look at my Retirement Key, you'll notice "Technology" is something I hate. Here's the thing, though: doing one of your Hates that you have to do counts as a Win.

And in honor of that hard fought Win, and because it was a beautiful evening, I treated myself to a nice, long walk around the neighborhood.

INSIGHTS

Celebrating Wins is healthy. It feels good. It boosts your confidence and self-esteem. It gives you the feeling of having a successful day, which is huge. Because a successful retirement is built on having successful days.

Becoming skilled with this Tool adds a little pep to your step. And as the story in this chapter has shown, there's an amazing synergy that can be created with celebrating Wins, taking your 3 Steps, and using your Retirement Key.

So far, in Part 2, I've introduced you to a handful of Tools and I've explained how to use them safely. Now, it's time for you to get acquainted with your advanced power Tools—2 of the 3 Ps you need to stay young.

CHAPTER 14

A Brief Interlude...
Passion and Purpose

L ET'S PAUSE FOR A moment and review what you've learned in Part 2.

So far, we've talked about harnessing the same Tools that made you successful at work and utilizing them in your retirement. These include finding a good role model/mentor and making sure to take your 3 Steps each day. I also introduced you to your WishList and Retirement Key, gave you a safety talk on how to use them, and emphasized the importance of celebrating Wins.

Now, because I like to walk my talk, I want you to stop reading this chapter and go celebrate your Win of learning all of this. Don't worry. This book will be here, waiting for you when you come back. But for now, go do something nice for yourself.

Seriously.

I'm going to go make myself a mocha and put on some tunes. Because, honestly, writing this much of the book is a big accomplishment. So, I say we take the rest of this day off, go do things that we enjoy and make us feel good, and come back tomorrow all refreshed and recharged.

"GOOD MORNING, GOOD MORNING"

Alright, I hope you're feeling good because we've got some work to do today. Up until now, all the Tools I've shown you have been basic in nature. They're like your 100-level classes. Today, however, we're upping our game and getting into the advanced curriculum.

That's right. You've mastered the basics. Now it's time to break out the power Tools. The ones you've been using up until now are like protractors, rulers, and handsaws. Important. Necessary, even. But not exactly sexy.

The Tools coming up? These are your nail gun, drill, and chainsaw. These are the ones that will make your Plan in Part 3 sing. These are the Tools you're going to rely on when it comes to building yourself a retirement that feels good and lasts a long time.

TWO OF YOUR PS

As the title implies, and as I mentioned in Chapter 1, there are 3 Ps that will keep you young. They are: Passion, Purpose, and a Plan.

Passion and Purpose are non-negotiables. They are necessary components for any happy, successful retirement. Think of them as two load-bearing pillars. With them, your Plan at least has a fighting chance. Without them, even the best laid Plan is dead in the water—these Ps are that important.

And because they're so important, I'm going to teach you ways to include them in your Plan.

For this to happen, we need to make sure we're on the same page. We'll use the definitions of Passion and Purpose from Morten Hansen, a professor, author, speaker, and all-around smart guy. On episode #441 of *The Art of Manliness* Podcast, he said:

> Passion is doing what you love, whereas Purpose is doing what contributes. Passion is about what excites you, what the world can give you. Purpose is about what you can do for others. It is what you can give the world.

Pretty simple, right?

Your Passions are the things you do that give you life. They excite and energize you. And as Hansen says, there's an element of taking from the world that goes along with your Passions. They are about what you get.

Your Purposes, on the other hand, are about what you give. These are the things you do to contribute; they are focused on others. They may also excite and energize you, but that's not why you do them. You do them to be of service.

Now that we've come to terms with our terms—it's time to start digging in and using our Tools to build upon the groundwork we've done.

Get excited. The next chapter is all about uncovering, discovering, and connecting with your Passion.

CHAPTER 15

Passion

WELCOME TO YOUR FIRST advanced class—Passion 202. As I mentioned in the last chapter, and even earlier in the book, you need to have Passion in your life. It is literally vital energy—it keeps you alive. It's a crucial component in being happy and staying young.

Remember the definition we're using: Passion is the stuff you do for yourself. Making sure you have it in your life amounts to making sure you spend time doing the things you like to do, and leave you feeling happy.

This chapter will help you figure out what those activities are and how to get in touch with that ever-so-important feeling.

GETTING DIRTY

A client of mine, Gerald, wanted to retire at the age of 62. He came into my office to talk over his options after receiving some tragic news. His younger sister, Shelly, had been diagnosed with an aggressive cancer.

Hearing this, he immediately took a leave of absence from his job. While the higher-ups at his firm would surely miss the sixty hours a week Gerald worked, they weren't without heart. His bosses told him to take all the time he needed.

He was on a plane the next morning.

The first thing he noticed when he arrived at his sister's home was the state of her garden. Usually, Shelly was meticulous in the way she cared for it, to the point where it was a running joke in their family. "Oh? Shelly? She can't make it to your ninetieth birthday party, Mom. There are too many weeds to pull." Given how overgrown the garden was, Gerald knew the severity of the situation. There's no way Shelly would allow her garden to look like that if she could help it.

Gerald's brother-in-law, Scott, greeted him at the door.

"How is she?" Gerald asked.

"It's really turned ugly, Gerald. I'm glad you're here. Shelly's resting. She's been doing a lot of that lately."

Not knowing what to do, and not wanting to add stress to an already stressful situation, Gerald decided to work in the garden. This way, he was out of the way but helping. While gardening wasn't something he did often as an adult, it was something he and Shelly did a lot when they were kids.

As he was outside pruning overgrown plants and crawling on his hands and knees pulling weeds, Gerald found himself asking some very deep questions.

"What am I doing with my life?"

"What am I accomplishing?"

"Am I happy?"

"How would I enjoy spending the time I have left?"

The way Gerald tells it, these questions were vast and he spent the rest of the day lost. Both in the questions and in his sister's garden.

"The fact that I had no answers bothered me," he told me later. "It's like I'd been on autopilot my whole life and never checked in with myself. The only real plan I had was to work until I was 70, earn as much money as I could, max out my 401(k) and Social Security, and then retire.

"The next morning, I woke up and Shelly was feeling better. She and I spent most of the day reminiscing. We told stories and laughed. Most of the memories that came up were of us being kids in the garden. Later, when Shelly had to rest and recover from her treatment, I decided to make myself useful again by going outside and working in the garden.

"I was pleased with the progress I'd made the day before, both in the garden and in my thoughts, but there was so much more to do. I returned to the garden and my questions, only this time, when I got to 'What would make me happy?' an answer jumped out at me. Gardening. That's how I wanted to spend my time. And that's why I'm here today. Gary, I'm curious. Do I have enough money to retire and spend the rest of my life playing with plants?"

We went over the numbers. They looked good. Barring catastrophe or poor decision making, I told Gerald he should be able to maintain his current lifestyle.

"That's all I needed to hear. Thank you, Gary. This is exactly what I was hoping you'd say. That settles it. Tomorrow I'm giving my notice."

True to his word, Gerald did just that. Within two months, he went from working sixty-hour weeks to walking away from work entirely. Now, he spends his days outside, and I'm not sure he's ever been happier.

I ran into Gerald recently. He looked younger, more alive. "How's it going?" I asked. "How's the garden?"

"Gary," he said. "I'm so pumped. It's my first harvest so I don't know if it's going to be good or bad. But I know I'm going to learn a ton. And more importantly, I'm happy. There's nothing better than spending my days outside and playing in the dirt. It's the best."

FEELING IT

Call it energy or enthusiasm. Call it excitement or joy. These are all words describing the feeling I'm talking about. I call it Passion.

Whatever you choose to call it doesn't matter. Having it does.

Passion feels good. It's the energy of life and creation. It's the stuff that makes you feel like a kid again.

Keep that phrase in mind, "felling like a kid again," because that's what we're after. There's a good chance that's where your Passion lives. Getting you back to that place and in touch with that feeling is what the Tool is all about. That's why I call it "Growing Down."

Look—you're retired. That means you've officially done all the "growing up" you need to do. Now, it's time for you to start "Growing Down."

By this, I mean really getting back in touch with the

person you are at your core. To do this, we're going to do a little time traveling, back to the days of your youth.

When I was a kid, oh so very long ago, I spent hours and hours coloring. My mom loved that I enjoyed this. All she had to do was hand me a coloring book and some crayons and I amused myself. Which was great, because it meant I wasn't bothering her.

I think about this memory every time I see an adult coloring book in a bookstore. These are perfect examples of a product designed to help you Grow Down and reconnect with the youthful energy of Passion.

This idea of Growing Down is present in Gerald's story too, right there, hidden in plain sight. What were the words he used to describe how he spent his time in the garden? He used a phrase usually associated with children. He said he was "playing in the dirt."

Passion, this feeling we're talking about, is the root of Growing Down. It's enlivening. It's exciting. It's energetic. It's that feeling of being a kid again.

Maybe for you it was trains or cars. Maybe it was fashion or jewelry. Maybe it was painting or collecting bugs. Whatever it was, it was something.

GROWING DOWN

This process is designed to help you find your way back to being a kid again. It's a brainstorming/self-awareness exercise. This means going with the first answers that pop into your mind.

No second guessing.

No judging.

1. **You know the drill**—This Tool starts out like your WishList and Retirement Key. Go to your Thinking Place. Bring your writing supplies. No timer needed.

2. **Ask yourself**—When is the last time you felt like a kid? What were you doing?

3. **Ask yourself**—What are some other things you enjoyed doing when you were a kid?

MY ANSWERS

The last time I felt like a kid again, I was drinking a milkshake. There's an ice cream stand called Kustard Korner. They make a killer hot fudge milkshake. I've been drinking them for as long as I can remember. I'm not sure what it is about those shakes, but every time I drink one I feel like a kid again.

What I liked doing as a kid: Riding my bike, playing basketball, baseball, going to day camp, and sales. Yes. Sales. It might sound weird, but I've been selling things for as long as I can remember. It started with potholders. I used to make them and then go around the neighborhood door-to-door and sell them. Eventually, as I got older, potholders became fireworks, which were totally illegal and quite profitable. I think business has always been in my blood.

THE RUBBER MEETS THE ROAD

I took a client through this exercise and I absolutely loved her answer.

"This might sound strange," she said, "but I've always loved loud music. When I was seven, my older brother got the forty-five of 'Nights in White Satin.' Immediately, I was hooked. When he went out with his friends, I'd sneak into his room, put on the record, turn it up as loud as it would go, and put my ear right next to the speaker."

"Really?" I asked. "I had no idea you were such a Moody Blues fan."

"Oh, definitely," she said. "That moment, the first time I heard 'Nights in White Satin,' was when I discovered my Passion for music. Now I go to concerts whenever I can. I don't even care what type of music it is, or that I'm old enough to be the musician's grandmother. Being at a concert and hearing loud music makes me feel like a kid again."

If Growing Down doesn't do the trick for you, I've got another Tool to tell you about.

UNPACKING YOUR PASSION

Thinking about the things you loved doing then and love doing now is one way to discover and connect with sources of Passion. But there are other ways. This one uses your WishList.

There's a reasonable chance some of your Passions are hiding on your WishList. If these are obvious to you, great. Circle them, jot them down, or make a note somewhere else. They'll come in handy later on.

If your Passions aren't there, staring you in the face and begging for your attention, then this next exercise is for you. It uses your WishList.

Until now, the Tools I've shown you have been geared toward brainstorming. This one, the Passion Filter, isn't. Here you're not so much "brainstorming" as you are "body feeling." It's not about coming up with new ideas, it's about evaluating the ones you've already had. To do this, you'll focus on the sensations in your body and a little old-fashioned gut wisdom.

It's your somatic reactions, not your thoughts, that will be your guide. Because it's here, in your body, where the clues and cues to your Passions lie.

If reading that last sentence made you uncomfortable, congratulations! Uncomfortable is a feeling. Recognizing feelings is an essential part of this Tool. So, that means you're actually ahead of the game. You've got nothing to worry about. You'll do great.

YOUR PASSION FILTER

1. **Take a guess**—Back to your Thinking Place. Go there. Bring your WishList, something to write with, and something to write on.

2. **Get ready**—Close your eyes. Take a couple of deep breaths. Get rid of as much internal chatter as you can.

3. **Open your eyes and read**—Now, quick. Say the first item on your Wishlist out loud. You don't have to scream it, a whisper is fine.

4. **Pay attention to your body**—What did you notice in your body when you read your first item? What reaction did you have? Did saying it out loud give you a jolt of energy? Where? Did it spark an emotion? Which one? Was it excitement? Did you get chills? Goosebumps? Did saying it put a damper on your system? Did you yawn? Feel depleted? Whatever your reaction—make a note of it.

5. **Onto the next one**—Now, repeat what you just did for each item on your WishList. Be sure to give yourself enough time to reset between each item. Returning your body to neutral is the only way to get an accurate read. If you don't allow your body to reset before moving onto the next item, you run the risk of confusing your new reaction with the previous one.

WHAT JUST HAPPENED

Some bodily responses are easy to decipher. Goosebumps, chills, a burst of energy, increased heart rate, your mind racing with excitement, feelings of joy or happiness—these are no-brainers. They are all signs of Passion.

Likewise, if you noticed your body tightening up, your hands or feet clenching, your brow furrowing, your shoulders scrunching, yawning, sadness, or an overall draining of your energy—these indicate what you said out loud isn't a Passion.

Did saying an item from your WishList make you feel tired or drained?

This is almost a surefire sign that what you read aloud isn't a Passion. While anxiety and excitement are basically the same feelings, only with a different story attached to each of them, tiredness is the opposite of excitement and energy.

Finally, I've got one more Tool you can use to help you Grow Down and discover where a Passion of yours might be hiding.

GO TO YOUR RETIREMENT KEY

Your Retirement Key provides you with another way to discover your Passions—your Loves.

Your Loves are a list of things you really enjoy doing. That means your Loves are probably closely linked to your Passions. Because remember the definition of Passion we're using: Passions are the things you do for yourself.

INSIGHTS

Hopefully, after reading Gerald's story and the others, you realize the importance of Passion. There's a reason it's the first P. It's necessary if you plan on retiring and being happy.

With any luck, between Growing Down, the Passion Filter, and your Retirement Key, you've been able to identify a handful of potential Passions. Keep this list handy. It's going to be very important moving forward as your Passions became a pillar of your Plan.

But before we jump ahead to Part 3 and work on putting together your Plan, there's one other pillar, the second P we need to cover—Purpose. The Tools in the next chapter, the last in Part 2, are devoted to helping you cultivate your Purpose, the things you do for others.

CHAPTER 16

Purpose

READY TO LEARN ABOUT the last Tool you'll need before you're finally ready to start building your Plan? Good. I was hoping you'd say that.

Welcome to Purpose 202!

Purpose, along with Passion, is something you have to build into your life in order to retire and stay young. Many of us use "work" to meet this all-important need. And that makes sense, given the definition we're working with.

Remember, Purpose—for our purposes—is being defined as: "the things you do for others." "Work" is a nice and easy entry point into this place of service. But now that you're retired...

This is what brings us to this chapter. Here, we're going to take a little time to get you back in touch with Purpose.

PLAYING WITH PURPOSE

Some of you will have zero trouble identifying your Purpose. For some of you, it's likely something obvious, something you've thought about previously, and something you're already invested in. You are the lucky ones.

Take a moment and congratulate yourself. Seriously. Having Purpose is a huge Win. It is, after all, one of the 3 Ps you need for a happy and successful retirement. Go celebrate!

If, on the other hand, you happen to be on the other side of this coin, thinking to yourself, "What is my Purpose?" To you I say, fear not. Know that you've got lots of company and you're about to learn a couple of Tools to help you discover just that.

One of the first things I like to do when talking to people about Purpose is consult their WishList. I know. "But, Gary, everything seems to revolve around my WishList..." Yeah, well, that's why you made it.

1. **Pull out your WishList**—Read over what's there. Did something else just pop into your mind that you should add? Great! This is a perfect time for that.

2. **Pull it apart**—Break your WishList down into broad categories. General themes are what you're looking for. Things like "Travel," "Hobbies," "New Skills," etc.

3. **Like attracts like**—Now that you've got your themes, use them as headers. Put the items from your WishList into their relevant categories.

4. **It's about them**—Look at your categories. Do any focus on helping others? Remember, this exercise is all about Purpose, not Passion. We're looking to be of service, not to serve ourselves.

5. **Get yourself a mocha or a milkshake**—Discovering Purpose is a Win. Go celebrate.

In case you get confused, I went ahead and did this exercise too.

"USE ME"

Bill Withers, anyone? No? Ah, you're no fun...

TRAVEL	GOLF	CREATIVITY	TEACHING	LEARNING
Spend more time in Europe	Extraordinary Golf w/ Linda	Have a gallery showing of my paintings	Write a book of spiritual stories	Learn to play bongos
Visit all 50 States	Play 40+ rounds/year	Start painting	Write a best-selling book	Attend a writer's conference
Riverboat down the Mississippi and Rhine	Play Bandon Dunes w/ Linda	Write a song	Write a successful blog about retirement	Start/join a book club
See the Canadian Capitals	Pinehurst w/ Linda		Keynote Speaker	Take a basic technology course
MLB Stadiums / Road games			Teach financial principles to youth	
Visit more National Parks			Mentor a new financial advisor	
Visit Sedona, AZ, Charleston, SC, Etc.			Go on a speaking/ book tour	
Pacific Northwest and Napa Valley				
Train across the Canadian Rockies				
Music Cruise				

Looking at my WishList, there are five main categories.

- **Traveling**—Far and away the largest. I didn't even list all of the items, that's how big it is.

- **Golfing**—Four items on my list have to do with hitting that little maddening ball.

- **Creating**—Evidently there's an artist in here somewhere. Take that, Mr. Hamilton. Telling me in second grade to stop coloring outside the lines...

- **Teaching**—Seven items on my WishList revolve around passing information along to others.

- **Learning**—There are four items pertaining to gaining new skills.

Okay, so, golf, travel, creating, and learning aren't Purpose. These are all about me, which means they're Passions—one of the 3 Ps that will keep you young, but not the one we're looking for here.

However, the items listed under teaching? That's what we're after. Sharing the hard-fought lessons and wisdom I've learned? That's serving others, That's giving back. That's Purpose.

Writing books is a way for me to add Purpose, the second P, to my life. Putting what I've learned in print helps me to reach a greater audience than teaching a class. All the effort it takes to write a book, and believe me it takes plenty, keeps me in touch with my Purpose.

Sharing everything I've learned about how to retire, helping you lay your foundation, giving you these Tools, showing you how to use them, and building a Plan that suits you—this is all me, working with Purpose.

PURPOSE + PASSION = A 303 CLASS

Lining up your 2 Ps, your Passion and Purpose, isn't nearly as difficult as you might think. My favorite way of doing it is by cross-referencing your WishList and Retirement Key.

What you're looking for is the overlap between any of your Loves (or, failing that, your Likes) and the categories from your WishList that involve serving others.

Using me as an example...

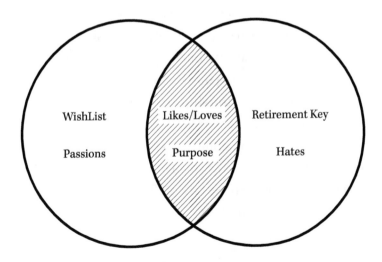

Right there, plain as day, "Solving problems," "Sharing what I've learned," and " Helping others" are a few of my Loves.

These essentially boil down to the same thing as "teaching" on my WishList. It's marrying my Passion (some of my Loves) with Purpose (the things I do for other people).

And with any luck, this will be how it works for you too. There will be places where the things you like to do for yourself overlap with how you can help others. Once you have an idea of where this is, where these first 2 Ps intersect, then you need to make sure those activities become part of the third P, your Plan.

INSIGHTS

Remember, Purpose is the thing you do for others, and it's important as part of your retirement.

In this chapter, I showed you a way to use two of the Tools you've previously learned to find places of Purpose.

This is by no means the only way to add Purpose to your life. As you'll see moving into Part 3, there are other, more traditional ways (mentorship and volunteering come to mind), you can meet this need.

And with that, congratulations! You've officially graduated from the Gary Sirak School of Retirement Tools. See you next chapter where we kick off Part 3, bring everything together, and begin building your Plan.

PART 3

CHAPTER 17

Putting It All Together

FIRST THINGS FIRST. IF you haven't already, or better yet, if you want to again, celebrate your Win for having made it all the way to Part 3.

Welcome to your Plan, the third and final P that will keep you young.

We'll start off by going over what all good Plans have in common, then it's on to a quick reminder of why your Plan is so important, before finally settling in on how to build yours. We'll go piece by piece, using your Tools from Part 2. And when we're finished, you'll have your Plan in your hands, complete with ideas for how to carry it out.

Carrying out your Plan starts with the 3 Steps. That's the framework you're going to use for your schedule. And your schedule is the framework, the structural support, of your Plan.

After covering all things schedule related, I'll take you through how to determine the best Steps for you. This is the bulk of what remains in this book. I'm not going to lie. There is some work ahead. Figuring out your Steps takes a bit of effort. But, hey, on the upside, it comes with a pool. I bet you didn't know you'd get one of those in this book...

Then, putting together everything you've learned, you'll be ready to build your Plan. You'll be equipped to choose the right Steps. And with any luck, have a nice, long retirement.

Doesn't sound too bad, does it?

Before moving on, I want to give you a glimpse of what a successfully executed Plan looks like. Your specifics may vary. The principles do not.

"A DAY IN THE LIFE"

Six months ago, one of my Steps for the day was to return a phone call. One of my oldest friends, Roy, and I had been trading calls and missing each other for weeks. From the voicemails he left, I knew he was cooking something up.

The previous year, Roy and his wife, Janet, met Linda and I in Las Vegas. We had a blast. It was a weekend full of great food, good shows, a little bit of gambling, and a whole lot of laughs. Because the four of us traveled so well together and had as much fun as we did, I had my fingers crossed Roy was planning our next adventure.

I managed to get Roy on the phone. After our obligatory discussion of Cleveland sports, we got down to business.

"Janet and I were talking and we both agreed, you and Linda are our favorite travel partners. What would you say to another trip? This time, it's going to be a tour of Canyon Lands National Parks with Tauck Tours. They're a first-class outfit. And the best part—you're going to love this, Gary—I've already researched all the hotels and flights. All you and Linda have to do is say yes, pay for it, and show up."

I laughed.

"Roy, you know me too well. This sounds perfect. Send me all the dates and details. I'll run it by Linda and let you know tomorrow."

As soon as I hung up the phone, I was elated. Why?

1) My WishList

Right there, plain as day, was "Visit more National Parks." Because it's on my WishList, that means it's something I want to do, which means it meets my need for the first P, Passion.

2) My Retirement Key

"Booking travel" has always been one of my least favorite things to do, a Hate for sure. But, lucky for me, Roy loves booking travel. Finding hotels, looking at menus for restaurants, and researching fun activities to do are things he genuinely enjoys doing. So, traveling with Janet and Roy meant I didn't have to spend a second on one of my Hates.

And "Crossing things off lists," "Traveling," and "Staying in touch with friends" are all Loves.

3) My 3 Steps

Calling Roy back was a Step for that day. Doing a Step is a Win. After I hung up the phone with him, I only needed two more for my day to be a success.

4) Celebrating Wins

Let's count up all my Wins from this single Step:
  · One for returning the call, the Step I had scheduled.

- Making plans to do something on my WishList is another.

- Travel with friends while not spending time doing one of my Hates definitely counts.

"How did I celebrate all these Wins?" you ask. I decided to take Linda out to our favorite ice cream shop, Kustard Korner, for hot fudge milkshakes.

INSIGHTS

This one example illustrates how using your Tools from Part 2 to design your Plan can work. On display are my WishList, Retirement Key, 3 Steps, celebrating Wins, and Passion—all of which were contained in a single Step, a simple phone call.

This is what Part 3 is about. It walks you through how to take what you've learned so far and use it to create a structure for your retired life. That's really what your Plan is, a schedule of Steps that meets your needs and works for you.

That's a critical component to living your marathon.

Now, we're going to spend a minute or two going over what makes a Plan a good one.

CHAPTER 18

Three Things
Every Good Plan Needs

YOUR PLAN IS GOING to be unique. It's going to be different than mine, your neighbor's, or anyone else's. This
makes sense. Retirement isn't one size fits all. There isn't
a "right way," there's only a right way for *you*.

That said, while the specifics of your Plan will be different than Debbie's or Ben's across the street, there are some
common threads all good Plans share. Plans, in a way, are
like jackets.

All jackets are meant to cover your upper body, include
sleeves, and are made from some sort of material. No material and it's nothing. No sleeves and it's a vest. And if it's
made for your legs, then it's one of any other number of
garments, none of which are "a jacket."

So, much like there are three things every jacket needs in
order to be a jacket, there are three things every Plan needs
in order to be successful. How you combine those things is
what makes it yours and unique.

The first thing you have to do with your Plan is make
sure it includes something to look forward to each day. This

sounds so fundamental and basic it should go without saying, but a shocking number of retirees seem to forget this simple fact. Infusing each day with moments of joy and satisfaction is hugely important. It's one of the reasons I'm so passionate about tracking and celebrating Wins.

Speaking of Passion, that's something else all good Plans share. You'll want to make sure you've got plenty of that first P. Same goes for Purpose. These are the pillars of your Plan. It's what holds it up. Without them, your Plan is doomed to fall apart.

Lastly, every good Plan I've ever seen fulfills your needs, especially the ones you previously met through work. Because again, the fact you're no longer working doesn't mean these needs magically disappear. It just means you're on the hook to figure out new ways of meeting them. And if your Plan doesn't achieve that, then it's probably not so good.

Now, knowing the requirements of every good Plan, it's time to create yours—one custom made and tailored to your particular situation, circumstances, and life.

A PLAN THAT FITS

To review, there are four major benefits we get from work: money, social connections, identity/value/worth, and structure. As for how much of each one of these you need, that depends.

- **Money**—This need might be satisfied by your 401(k), Social Security, and any additional assets you've accumulated along the way. If it isn't, then a part-time job might be in order.

- **Social Connections**—This need can be met in any number of ways. Maybe it's meeting friends for coffee, lunch, or a game of pickleball. Perhaps it's through a hobby you enjoy, a place you volunteer, or babysitting your grandkids.

- **Identity/Value/Worth**—This one is trickier. If you are the type of person who strongly identified with your occupation, then this may require major attention. I've seen some people solve this problem by getting involved with local organizations in a leadership capacity. Another option is mentoring. The more Steps you take infused with Purpose and helping others, the better for your sense of value, worth, and identity.

- **Structure**—This could be the most stressful aspect of your new normal, especially if you're someone who liked your old job and routine. Lucky for you, structure is what we're covering here in Part 3. We're building your schedule, your Plan, as a way of satisfying this need.

DOING MEANINGFUL THINGS

The second target you're aiming for revolves around what you learned at the end of Part 2. You need to make sure you've got your 2 Ps covered. Your Plan has to include Steps you take for you (Passion) and ones you take for other people (Purpose).

Having both of these as part of your retirement Plan goes a long way toward making it meaningful and keeping you young.

MAKE IT FUN

One of the easiest ways to make sure your Plan includes enough fun is by choosing Steps involving Passion. This means pursuing activities from your WishList along with Likes and Loves from your Retirement Key. Another way to add a little fun to your Plan is by celebrating your Wins.

IDEALLY EACH DAY WILL LOOK LIKE THIS

- **Schedule three different things for yourself**—These are your Steps. We'll go over how to choose the right ones for you soon.

- **Each Step you take is a Win**—Wins are good. Getting at least three a day is your goal.

- **Every Win deserves to be celebrated**—Do something nice for yourself or others in honor of your accomplishment. It doesn't have to be big or grand. It can be a simple, "Nice job, Gary!" or "Woo!" Another favorite, non-beverage celebration is doing one of my Loves—"Crossing things off lists." I get so much pleasure from taking a pen and putting a simple line through something on a list.

This is the general overview of what your retired life is going to look like. This is the basic outline of your Plan.

Take 3 Steps a day. The Steps you decide to take are up to you.

If you're an introverted night-owl, then your 3 Steps will look a lot different than the ones for a sun-worshipping social butterfly. That's the beauty. It's made to order.

HOW TO TELL IF YOUR PLAN FITS

One of the surest ways to determine if you've built a good Plan is to check in with yourself. If you feel satisfied and fulfilled at the end of your day, then congratulations. There's a solid chance you've built a good Plan and executed it well.

If, at the end of the day, you feel exhausted but happy, that's a good sign.

If, at the end of the day, you feel content, that also works.

But let's face it—the real world is not nirvana. You will have bad days. Maybe you had to devote an entire day to doing your Hates. Perhaps you or a loved one is ill. Whatever the case may be, on those nights when you're feeling less than stellar and dissatisfied, my advice is to let it go.

The truth is, every day can't be the best day, regardless of how well-designed your Plan is. That's not the way the world works. The only thing you can do after a frustrating day is sleep it off and start over again tomorrow.

However, if you're regularly feeling depleted and down, then you should probably start tinkering with your Plan. There's a reasonable chance either your needs have changed, or the Steps you've chosen to meet them aren't doing the trick.

INSIGHTS

All good Plans have three things in common. They meet your needs, are full of Passion, and have plenty of Purpose. So, in order for your Plan to be good and to keep you young, you need to make sure your Plan has all three.

Use the 3 Steps. This Tool takes care of your need for structure.

How you meet your other needs (money, social connections, value/worth/identity, passion, and purpose) is up to you.

Unfortunately, there isn't an app or a professional you can consult to determine if the Plan you've made for yourself is working. The only way to know is to check in with yourself and be honest.

If it is, then perfect!

If it's not, that's also perfect! Remember Chapter 6 and your Retirement Mindset from Part 1. Be grateful for the feedback you've gotten, come back, and reread the chapters necessary to improve your Plan.

Oh, and if you're still not convinced you need to have a Plan, let the two stories in the next chapter serve as a reminder.

CHAPTER 19

Family Time

THERE ARE MANY WAYS to exit this planet. The one I've witnessed most often is being "bored to death." But there are other ways.

One, of course, is murder. A detective friend told me most violent crimes are committed by people the victim knows. And, since this book is about how to retire and not die, I thought it fitting to include a chapter about how to retire and not be murdered by a family member.

If you're like most people "spending more time with family," is likely part of your Plan. As we've discussed, social connections are one of your needs, and making sure your needs are being met is part of any good Plan. So, meeting your social needs with family is smart.

Know what else is smart? Making sure your family is on the same page. Because newsflash—they might not be.

Take these two tales as evidence. Both happened in the same week. And both serve as a really good reminder as to why having a Plan is so important.

GOING GROCERY SHOPPING

I decided to run to the store. It was the middle of the afternoon, and one of the banks I use has a branch inside a supermarket. I needed to make a deposit, plus I was out of whipped cream. And as a mocha lover, that wasn't going to fly.

Walking toward the grocery store, I heard someone call my name. Turning, I saw long-time clients, the Mitchells, waving and walking my way.

Greg and Anne had been in my office about a month ago to talk about retirement. Greg was a rock star real estate investor who had earned many, many dollars during his career. He had built his successful commercial real-estate development business from scratch and was used to hustling, making hard decisions, and not taking no for an answer.

Following our brief chat in the parking lot, we went our separate ways. I went to the bank. They went to buy groceries.

After making my deposit, I set out to find the whipped cream. Walking by the cookie section, I heard a rather angry, "Put that back!"

The voice I recognized. The tone I did not.

Glancing down the aisle, I saw Greg holding a package of Oreos. He looked sheepish. Anne, meanwhile, was shaking her head.

"C'mon" I heard him say. "What's the big deal? I haven't had these since I was a kid. I used to love Oreos."

"No," said Anne, "These are NOT on your diet." After an exasperated sigh, she continued, "This, this is why I didn't want you to come shopping. You always do this, you act like a 4-year-old. This is why I told you to stay home."

"But I didn't have anything else to do. I was bored out of my mind sitting there, flipping channels. I figured doing something was better than doing nothing."

"Greg" she said in the most patient voice she could muster. "We talked about this. Hanging out with me and following me around is not a retirement plan."

I heard Greg start to protest but decided I'd lingered for long enough. It was time to move on. The whipped cream was calling.

Returning from the dairy department, I peeked down the cookie aisle. There was Greg, looking defeated. His shoulders were slumped. His head was down and he still had the package of Oreos in hand. It was the saddest scene I'd witnessed in some time.

Not wanting to be caught, I kept walking toward the cashiers while thinking to myself, "Wow. Three months ago, this guy was running a multi-million dollar company, making all sorts of high-leverage decisions, and now he's got nothing better to do than get yelled at by his wife in the grocery store."

Which brings me to our second story.

THE DEADBOLT SOLUTION

Kathy and Bob have been friends and clients for over twenty years. We have spent countless hours golfing, traveling, and dining together. So, when I saw them on my appointment schedule for Thursday, I smiled.

They walked in together, which was strange. In all the time I'd known them, Kathy had only been to the office once.

"Gary, we're so glad you were able to meet with us. There's something we're really excited about and wanted to tell you in person."

While it was obvious Bob was excited, one glance at Kathy told me a very different story. All I got from her was a sense of cold. Not normal for Kathy. Usually, she was as bubbly and warm as they come.

Bob continued. "A large competitor wants to buy my company. Not only do they want to buy it, but they made me an offer for more money than I'd ever dreamed I could get for it. So, I'm thinking I should take the money and run."

Meanwhile, Kathy was dead silent. Not a peep. She was just staring down at the table, something clearly bothering her. At the time, I didn't know what.

"Bob, that's great! When's this all going to happen?" I asked.

"In three months," he says, "How incredible is that? I'm going to be a man of leisure with more money than I know what to do with. The people buying me out are the real deal. They've already agreed to retain my employees."

From here, the rest of the meeting proceeded as planned. I walked them through my pre-retirement questions. After reviewing their finances, it was apparent money wasn't going to be a problem, especially with the sale of Bob's company. This meant I got to jump ahead to my favorite line of questioning.

"Bob, the money checks out," I said. "You've got enough to retire and that's no small thing. Now, what I want to know is, what are you going to do with all your newfound time? You've worked six days a week for as long as I've known you. What are you going to do to keep busy?"

He hemmed and hawed. "Well...you know...I haven't really thought much about it. But I'll figure it out. Money is what's important. I'll have plenty of time to figure out what to do with my time later. How hard could it be?"

At this point, Kathy, who is one of the sweetest people you'll ever meet, and who hasn't said a word the whole meeting, did something I never dreamed she'd do in a million years. She hauled off and slugged Bob on the arm.

This wasn't a love-tap. It was a swing Muhammad Ali would have been proud of. The sound of her punch echoed around the room.

Bob was stunned. "What was that for?"

"I've told you from the beginning, when you first started talking about the sale. You need to find something to do. You keep telling everyone you'll figure it out. Well, that's not good enough and I'm sick of hearing it."

Bob, confused and rubbing his arm, stared at this wife.

"I don't want you screwing up my life," she continued. "I have my own life. I can see how this is going to go. I'm fine for breakfast. I'm fine for dinner. But you're not going to hang around and mess up all my days."

And with that, Kathy stormed out, officially marking the end of our meeting.

Fast forward.

The company sells. The money is in the bank. Kathy and Bob decide to celebrate with a two-week trip to Europe. By all appearances, everything seems to be working out. But looks, as you know, can be deceiving.

When Bob gets back into town, we meet for coffee.

"Thank you so much, Gary," he says. "If it weren't for you, I'm not sure any of this would have worked out."

"My pleasure, Bob. Helping people is what I do. How was the trip?"

"Oh, it was so nice, Gary. We did everything we wanted to. We spent five days in Italy, five days in France, and five in London. Amazingly, the weather was perfect the whole time. We ate so much good food and drank so much good wine. It's the retirement trip I always wanted to take."

"I'm happy for you and Kathy. What's the first non-vacation day of retirement have in store for you, Bob?"

"You're looking at it," he says. "All I had on my agenda was meeting with you. After this, I figured I'd head home, read the paper, and enjoy a nice day off."

We finish our coffee, finish our conversation, and go our separate ways.

Two weeks later, Bob calls again. He wants another coffee date. We settle on a place.

I grab my mocha and take a seat. The first thing I notice is Bob's appearance. He looks okay. Not great. But okay.

"What's on your mind, Bob?" I ask. "How's retirement treating you?"

He shakes his head. "Let me tell you what happened after you and I met the last time. I went home. I parked my car in the garage, but the door to the house was locked." He pauses and looks up, disbelief on his face.

"I don't keep a house key on my car keys. Kathy and I always leave that door unlocked. That's how we've always done it, unless we're away on vacation. I was surprised and confused, so I knocked. A couple of minutes later, the door opens and Kathy's standing there, hands on hips, glaring down at me. She doesn't say a word. She just stands there staring."

I take a sip of my mocha. "That doesn't sound good."

"I know. So I ask her, 'Why's the door locked?' And she says, 'Because you're not coming in.' 'But…I live here,' I say. Then she starts, 'Not during the day, you don't. I married you for better or worse. Not for lunch.' I was speechless. I didn't know what to say."

"What happened next?" I asked.

"She hands me a pad of paper and a pen. 'Here,' she tells me, 'Go figure out how you're going to spend your time. Dinner's at 7.' I think to myself, 'She's got to be kidding,' and I ask her as much."

"'You think I'm kidding?' she asks. 'I've never been more serious.' She slams the door and I hear the deadbolt click."

"Wow, Bob. That's quite the story. What did you end up doing?"

"Honestly? I stood there for what seemed like an eternity. Eventually, I made my way to the McDonald's down the street from the house. I sat there in shock. After a while, I pulled out the paper and pen Kathy practically threw at me and started writing."

"How'd it go?" I asked.

"The first note I wrote to myself was easy. It was: add a house key to my key ring. After that, I didn't know what to write. I was angry, but I knew she was right. I needed to figure out what the hell I was going to do with all of my time. Eventually, some ideas started to pop into my head. After a couple hours, I had a pretty good list."

"Well, that's good," I said.

"Yeah, tell me about it. That evening, I went back home and the door was unlocked. Without a word, I walked in and handed Kathy my list. She looked it over. As she got to the end, she gave a satisfied nod and handed it back to me."

"Did she say anything?"

"Yeah. 'Dinner's on the table.'"

INSIGHTS

Now, did Anne or Kathy actually have murder on their minds? No. Of course not. But the points I wanted to illustrate remain.

Sitting at home, watching TV, and hanging out with your spouse is not a Plan.

You need a real Plan. Just ask Greg or Bob.

None of your friends want to accidentally witness you and your spouse arguing in the grocery store.

The people you're planning on spending time with as part of your retirement might have their own, sometimes very strong, thoughts about that.

Clearly, Kathy did. She'd been living her own life for thirty plus years. She had her own routines and didn't want to change them. It's not that she didn't love Bob. If anything, it's *because* she loved him so much, she knew he needed to figure out his own life. Bob was so concerned about retiring, he never stopped for a second to consider how it might affect him and those around him when he did.

It's the same story with Greg and Anne.

Now that you know why a Plan is so important, let's start making yours.

CHAPTER 20

Knowing Your Needs

IN PART 2, YOU learned about my personal scheduling philosophy, the 3 Steps.

One of my favorite parts of the 3 Steps is it's an easy way to stay busy without burning out. No doubt, wrestling time management and exhaustion is something you did enough of during your working days. That's something best left in the past.

My second favorite part of the 3 Steps is the way it synergizes with your other Tools, specifically celebrating Wins. Every Step you take is a Win. Every Win you get is worthy of celebrating. Every celebration can be a Step. There's a rhythm here. Catch it and you fall into a virtuous cycle of feeling good about yourself and your life.

If you need a more in-depth refresher on this scheduling Tool, flip back to Part 2. Re-read Chapter 9.

Speaking of scheduling, I'd like to zoom out for a second. Every schedule is a combination of two parts—a *what* and a *when*. Making a mocha at noon. Going for a walk after dinner. Playing bongos when Linda is outside in her garden. These are all a *what* and a *when*.

Again, not rocket science.

Making the right schedule for you amounts to choosing the best Steps and the best time to take them. That's it. That's the scaffolding of your Plan.

Choosing your best *whats* and *whens* means knowing yourself really well. Here, you'll learn about the best *whats* for you. The *whens* we'll cover in the next chapter.

A REFRESHER

Remember, the whole idea behind this book is: work meets more of our needs than we give it credit for. And even though work has gone away, your needs haven't. Now, it's up to you to learn how to meet them without work.

But here's the thing. It's really, really, really hard to meet your needs if you don't know what they are. So, in choosing your Steps, you must first be crystal clear about your needs. For that to happen, a little Part 1 and 2 review is in order.

Way back at the beginning of the book in Chapter 5, we talked about the needs you met with work. There were four main ones: structure, money, identity/value/worth, and social connections. In Part 2, I added two more needs to the list, the 2 Ps, Passion and Purpose.

That makes six total. Since Part 3 is basically one big masterclass on how to best meet your need for structure, we don't have to spend time reviewing that one. It's the other five I'd like to revisit before moving on.

MONEY

Sure, the best things in life are free. Unfortunately, everything else costs money. That didn't magically change since you decided to retire. So, money is a need you have to meet. For some, this will come from investments and savings. For others, it's not.

Being part of the second camp is nothing to be ashamed of; in fact, you have a lot of company. Many people need more money in order to make their retirement work. It's very common.

Living in the world costs a lot. Working part-time is a phenomenal Step for anyone in need of more cash. Each shift you work counts as a Step for the day and adds a few bucks to your coffers. Nothing wrong with that.

As for finding the right part-time job to fit you—hold tight. We'll get there.

IDENTITY/VALUE/WORTH

Many retirees I work with are hit with a feeling of loss when they retire. Part of this feeling of grief can come from having to let go of a core part of your identity. This has happened, to some degree, to almost every retiree I've ever met.

If you've lost that loving feeling of being important and needed, then be honest with yourself about it. As for what to do about it, well, that's not what we're doing here. Here you're identifying your needs, which is the first step to meeting them.

(Don't worry. I'll tell you the best way to meet this need later on).

SOCIAL CONNECTIONS

Co-workers provide many people with the interaction they need. And since you no longer have any co-workers, it's up to you to figure out new ways to fill this void. For now, all you want to do is identify your needs. We'll go over how to meet them later.

THE 2 PS

Passion and Purpose are critical pieces of the retirement puzzle. No matter who you are, no matter what other needs you do or don't have, you will need these Ps to create a successful, happy retirement.

Now that you've had a quick refresher, I've got an exercise to help you discover your needs. Fear not. It's easy. Besides, at this point, you're a pro.

GETTING TO KNOW YOUR NEEDS

1. **Go back to your Thinking Place**—Like you did when you put together your WishList, Retirement Key, Passion Filter, and other Tools. Take a piece of paper and something to write with.

2. **Make five headings**—Or use five different pieces. Just make sure you title each one with a different category of need (money, identity/value/worth, social connection, Passion, Purpose) and leave yourself plenty of space to write.

3. **Have at it**—Pick one need and start. "My needs for <blank> are…" Let it flow. Make sure to hit all five.

3.5. **If you're struggling**—Hop around. Not literally. I was thinking more of moving to a new category.

3.75. **Get Moving**—No, really. If you still feel yourself stuck and nothing is coming, then you could actually hop around. Or you can do what I do and take a walk instead.

4. **Set down your list**—Congratulations. Celebrate your Win. Treat yourself to a mocha. You've done what you need to do for today.

5. **Come back tomorrow**—Now, with rested eyes and in a refreshed state, review what you wrote. Read it again and see what jumps out at you. If it's all clear and concise—perfect. Awareness and clarity are what you're aiming for.

INSIGHTS

3 Steps a day. That's the schedule you're going to use to build your retirement. That's the scaffolding of your Plan.

And since it's your Plan, built from the ground up specifically for you, the schedule you create needs to reflect that.

All schedules are combinations of *whats* and *whens*.

That's why honing in on your needs is so important. Because if you don't know them, then you can't meet them.

And if you can't meet them, then...well...you remember what happened to Bruno.

With your needs clarified, you're in a much better position to start thinking about the *whats* you're going to choose to meet them. But remember, we're talking about your schedule, so it's not only about your *whats*.

It's also about your *whens*. That's right. Next chapter you'll learn about choosing the *whens* for your *whats*.

CHAPTER 21

The *Whens* For Your *Whats*

BEFORE GOING ANY FURTHER into the *whats of* your Plan, otherwise known as the Steps you're going to take to meet your needs, it's time to take a moment to think about *when*. Because, again, a schedule isn't only *what* you do but also *when* you do it.

Building a retirement that works for you means building a schedule that works for you. And as in the last chapter, this starts with knowledge. Previously, it was knowledge of your needs. Here, it's about recognizing your natural rhythms.

This might sound revolutionary or crazy, but I want you to construct your schedule, and thereby your Plan, around the way your body wants to operate. Natural rhythms, much like retirements, are also custom-built. Some of us need more sleep than others. Some find it easier to be creative and energized at 10 p.m., not at 10 a.m.

It amazes me how few of us are genuinely tuned into our bodies. Things as elementary as how much we need to sleep or eat remain mysteries. Some of us don't have a clue when our energy is at its peak, or when it winds down.

And just like knowing your needs is the first step to meeting them, knowing yourself and the way you operate is the first step in figuring out when it's the best time to meet them. It starts with self-awareness.

THINK BACK

Most of your life has been spent on someone else's schedule.

Take waking up. Beginning with school, there was a bus and a bell dictating when you had to be where. Next, it was a clock to punch at work. Then, perhaps, it was screaming infants and young children, wide awake and raring to go at 5:55 in the morning, or a dog that had to go out. In each instance, something or someone woke you up at a certain time.

Is food any different? Have you ever taken the time to tune into your body and eat when you were actually hungry? Or have you been eating when you've been told your entire life? Is three meals a day what's best for you? Is breakfast the most important meal of your day?

(For me, it is. But maybe not for you.)

All I'm pointing out is how likely it is you've been doing the basic, necessary actions of life on a schedule you were given, not one you chose.

We're building your ideal retirement here. Any ideal retirement is one that operates in tune with your ideal schedule. And in order to learn what that means for you, you'll have to get in touch with your body.

WAIT, YOU WANT ME TO WHAT?!
STOP.

You read that right.

I want you to stop.

Stop setting an alarm.

Stop eating when you're supposed to.

Stop allowing external influences to get in the way of your internal clock.

The beautiful thing about retirement is its freedom. You, not your boss or your company, decide the best time to do things. Although, if you have a partner or spouse, they might have a feeling or two about this.

I'm not telling you to stay awake and fast for seventy-two hours while lying around doing nothing. No. I'm asking you to rest, reset, and tune into when your body wants to do the things it needs to do.

Be active. Continue to live your life and start doing it according to the way your body wants to operate.

It may take time. Learning new things about yourself is a process. Some clients have taken a couple weeks. Others have taken a few months to wrap their arms around their natural rhythms. And like these rhythms themselves, how long it takes you to find yours will vary.

Over time, as you pay attention, you'll begin to notice your rhythms. You'll wake up when you're rested. You'll go to sleep when you're tired. You'll eat when you're hungry and you'll have a much better sense of when you're the most active, energized, and at your best.

After you figure out your sweet spots, you can build a schedule, a Plan, to genuinely work with them, and have them work for you.

INSIGHTS

Just because this chapter is short doens't mean it's not important. Ringo is only 5' 6" and he was the backbone of the best band of all time.

You are being given a gift, one you worked your whole life to be able to afford. One you climbed a metaphorical mountain to achieve, so please, take some time to get to know yourself and live the best marathon you can.

Learn *when* it's the best time to do the things you need to do.

You've been programmed and conditioned to go, go, go. This is what allowed you to make it this far.

But now that you're here, it's time to shift gears. This means paying attention to your body and pacing yourself.

This also means being a responsible human. Talk to your partner, spouse, or anyone else this radical departure is possibly going to impact. Preferably before you pull the plug on all your old routines.

Explain what you're doing and why. The conversation that follows could prove very interesting and illuminating.

Then—

Sleep when you're tired.

Eat when you're hungry.

Wake up when you're rested.

Do things when you're energized, and when it makes sense to do them.

And, whatever it looks like, go with it.

Learn the way you naturally operate.

It's likely going to take some time, and that's okay.

Figuring this stuff out matters. You're on the cusp of building your Plan, the thing we've been working toward since you cracked open this book.

Once you know more about your *whens*, it's time to look again at what sorts of activities you'll choose to be your 3 Steps for each day.

Fortunately, I've got some thoughts about that.

Get your swimsuit, grab a towel, and don't forget to lather on the sunscreen, because next chapter, we're heading to the Pool.

CHAPTER 22

Welcome To Your Pool

I BET YOU THOUGHT there'd be more water.
Unfortunately, that's not the type of "pool" we're talking about. The Pool we're dealing with is more along the lines of a "talent pool" or a "pool of competitors." It's "pool" as in a collection. I know. Sorry for getting your hopes up.

But, hey—on the upside—there's no need to chlorinate or clean the filters on this one. Plus you can run all you want and drink out of glass containers!

Now that you have a better sense of what your needs are and the best times to meet them, let's dive a little deeper into the Steps you'll take to do just that.

Steps, it turns out, are like water. They too come in two main categories. Only instead of salt water and fresh water, you've got Recurring and Once-in-a-while Steps. These names are pretty self-explanatory. Recurring Steps happen regularly. Once-in-a-while Steps happen every so often.

COMMON SOURCES FOR YOUR RECURRING STEPS

The Recurring Steps you'll use to build your Plan come from three main sources. These are: the hobbies you're interested in, going back to work, and going back to work for free. Yes, you read that right.

Hobbies are an easy sell. I doubt I need to spend a lot of time convincing you that making time for the things you want to do is a good choice. Hobbies are one of the best ways to make sure you have enough of your first P, Passion.

Two-thirds of your Pool of potential Steps might be filled by going back to work. I know. I know. The whole point of being retired is you're finally allowed to stop working. But hear me out...

You know my thoughts on work and the many positive things it brings. And since a major requirement of retiring and not dying is making sure all of your needs are met, it's worth considering either a part-time job or volunteering as one of your Steps.

Working part-time gives you a lot. It's a Recurring Step offering you a place to be at a certain time, social interaction, and they even pay you to do it. Again, there's an odd but true connection some people experience between earning money and self-esteem. If you're one of these people, a part-time job might be your ticket off the self-worth struggle bus.

Going the volunteering route gives you the same benefits as a part-time job, minus the money. There's a very good chance it will also involve some sort of social interaction. Helping out with a cause you believe in also provides a sense of well-being and time well spent. Volunteering is the best way I know of to make sure there's enough of your second P, Purpose, in your Plan.

Before you scoff, do me a favor and at least think about it. Whether you're doing it for money (working part-time) or for free (volunteering), it turns out the easiest way to make sure some of your old work needs are met is to go back to work. On your terms, of course, so it works for you.

BEING SMART WITH YOUR RECURRING STEPS

Remember—you are in control.

Whether you're participating in a hobby, working, or working for free, you're doing it to meet your needs and make your life better. This means if at any point you start to feel as though it's *taking* away from and not *adding* to your life, then it's time to stop. You climbed a mountain to be here. Enjoy it.

With that all-important first rule of being smart with your Recurring Steps out of the way, here's the second: Use your Tools. Turn back to your Retirement Key, WishList, and Passion Filter. They are invaluable for figuring out what hobbies to pursue and where to work or volunteer. I'll walk you through the specifics of how to do this in the coming chapters.

For now, let's shift our focus to the other type of Steps you'll want to have in your Pool.

ONCE-IN-A-WHILE STEPS

Things like exercise, spending time with your friends and family, volunteering, working part-time, and your hobbies are all regular activities. Regular activities are good. They give you a sense of structure and stability.

But there are other types of activities to choose for your Steps too. I call these Once-in-a-while Steps. As the name implies, these are the activities you schedule and do on occasion.

Travel is a great example of a Once-in-a-while Step. Most people I know don't like being on the road all the time. They do, however, appreciate a get-away every now and then.

Same goes for a gourmet meal. There's nothing I love more than a cup of lobster bisque followed by a fresh Dover sole, deboned table-side, over some creamy parmesan risotto and asparagus. But every night? No way.

Another favorite Once-in-a-while Step of mine is to clean house, so to speak. If you're anything like me, you have a couple spots in your home where you stash stuff for later examination. Things like mail, solicitations, reading material—basically anything you didn't have time or energy to deal with ends up in one of these places. Clearing these out is another example of a Once-in-a-while Step.

A seasonal review of your Wins is also a Once-in-a-while Step. This is one I've done in both my personal and professional life for more than twenty years. There's nothing like reviewing your last three months and seeing how much you've accomplished to help you feel good about yourself.

Treat this like making your Retirement Key or your WishList.

SEASONAL WIN REVIEW

1. **Go to your Thinking Place**—As per usual, bring something to write with and on.

2. **Review your last three months**—Write down every single Win you had.

For me, my favorite place to reflect, which will come as no surprise whatsoever, is at a coffee shop. I order a mocha, sit down, reflect over the last three months of my life, and write down every Win I can remember.

Setting aside time to intentionally feel good by acknowledging all your accomplishments is a fantastic Step. It provides a jolt of self-confidence, good feelings, and momentum. Every time I do it, I find myself leaving the coffee shop with a big smile and a little more pep in my step. Although, come to think of it, it could be the caffeine and chocolate...

INSIGHTS

There are two types of Steps you can use to fill your Pool, Recurring and Once-in-a-while. Most people prefer a majority of their Steps to be Recurring and use Once-in-a-while Steps to add a little variety.

Many of your Recurring Steps will likely come from the hobbies you choose to explore and the places you decide to work or volunteer.

It's on you to create the Once-in-a-while Steps. Traveling and gourmet meals are two common ones. I offered you a couple examples of mine in this chapter. But at the end of the day, a successful retirement and Plan mean coming up with the right Once-in-a-while Steps to keep your life interesting and fun.

And that's your Pool.

Now, let's hop up on the diving board and plunge into the deep end of choosing good Steps.

Next up—Passion, hobbies, and play.

CHAPTER 23

Hobbies

B Y NOW, IF YOU'RE not fully aware of the importance of filling your days with meaningful activities you enjoy, I'm not sure what book you've been reading. Being busy—but not too busy—and taking Steps to meet your needs is how you retire and not die.

There's a reason I started this book with Bruno and Betty's story. He didn't do those things. He didn't have a Plan. And sadly, because of that, Bruno exited the planet way too early.

But that's not going to happen to you. Because you're reading my book, you've laid down the foundation in Part 1. You've learned how to use your Tools in Part 2. And you're halfway through Part 3, which means you know what it takes to make your Plan a good one.

Who knew retiring would be so much work?

The good news? You're almost done. Most of the difficult work is behind you. Come to think of it, let's agree to stop using the "w" word (at least for the rest of this chapter). There's been enough of that lately.

It's fun-time now.

Wasn't that one of the reasons you decided to retire in the first place? To have more fun? It's time to harvest the fruits of your labors. It's time to pursue your passions.

Welcome to the chapter on hobbies, home of the first P that will keep you young, Passion, and an important part of your retirement marathon.

Let's get to it.

GOOD GOD, GWEN

A few months ago, one of my physician clients came to my office. Gwen was close to retiring. She had plenty of savings, and barring something completely unexpected, was going to retire in style.

"Okay, Gwen, you've been practicing medicine for thirty-five years..."

"Actually, when you start adding up medical school and residency," she chimed in, "it's been longer."

"Alright, let's call it forty plus years practicing medicine. In all that time, have you developed any hobbies? What sorts of things would you like to do in your soon-to-be permanent time off?"

"Hobbies?" she asked, "You're kidding, Gary. I haven't had any time for hobbies. I'm a doctor. I'm a wife. I'm a mom. I'm a soccer grandma. Gary, where exactly was I supposed to find the time for hobbies?"

Smiling, I replied, "What about between 10 p.m. and midnight? Gwen, I get it. Time has been scarce. But that's going to change. I've got a question for you. After you've finished practicing medicine, what are you going to do? You're going to be on the hook for filling your time seven days a week. That's a lot."

"I'll be fine. I love to read and watch movies. I've got shelves of books I've never read and a Netflix queue with fifty films on it. When I imagine my ideal afternoon, it involves being curled up under a blanket with a good book or watching an old movie."

"You do realize we're talking about the rest of your life, not five hours on a Sunday, right? If you're sitting here and telling me your Plan when you retire is to read and watch movies for forty hours a week, then you have some serious thinking to do. You've been go-go-go your whole life. Now you're just going to pull the plug, sit on the couch, and eat chocolate chip cookies? Does that sound even remotely realistic?"

She didn't answer right away. She did wrinkle her brow and narrow her eyes. Then, she smiled. "What have you got against chocolate chip cookies?"

Although it took her some time, I'm happy to say after a year of trial and error Gwen figured out her retirement. She joined a book club and liked it so much she decided to start her own. Then, following her passion for movies, she started another club. This one meets on Wednesdays and watches the Classics. Add in some travel and grandkid stuff, and Gwen is happily living her marathon.

HONING IN ON YOUR HOBBIES

By this time I'm guessing you have a pretty good idea of what we're going to use to look for hobbies. That's right. It's time to refer back to your WishList.

It's likely you're going to find some hobbies sitting there waiting for you.

Let's flip back to Chapter 16 on Purpose in Part 2, using my WishList as an example. There you will find my WishList broken down into categories. Looking it over, do you notice any hobbies I could potentially use as Recurring Steps?

Travel jumps out at me. There's an entire sub-category devoted to it. Same for golf. And you'll notice there are some artistic, creative pursuits too, like learning to play an instrument, writing, and painting.

Of those five categories, "travel" is the least useful, even though it makes up a majority of my WishList. Going places is wonderful. But unless you have unlimited funds and time, "travel," as I said in the last chapter, is a Once-in-a-while Step. For our purposes here, I'd like to focus on the hobbies from my WishList that can become Recurring Steps.

Tossing out "Travel" leaves me with "Playing golf," "Writing books," "Painting," and "Learning to play bongos." Those are all hobbies I could turn into Recurring Steps. They are activities I could realistically do at least once, if not a couple times each week as a part of my Plan.

Take a minute and go through your own WishList. Ignore the Once-in-a-while Steps and look for the categories you could turn into Recurring ones.

Now, it's time to put some thought into which hobby or hobbies to try first.

If you look over your WishList and there's something screaming, "Pick me! I'm the hobby you want!" pay attention to your intuition and see how it goes.

For me, it was learning to play the bongos. Am I any good at playing them? God, no. I'm horrendous. I just started. But I'm having fun and learning. Plus, it turns out beating on drums is a great way to relieve a little frustration. Who knew?

If, however, no hobby seems to be calling your name, keep reading. Below are some thoughts and questions to help you sift through your WishList and find a good starting point.

A quick word of caution…Remember Chapter 12 "The Safety Talk," from Part 2? Try before you buy. Just because 9-year-old you used to love riding your bike doesn't mean 69-year-old you will too.

SOCIALIZING

How are you going to manage your social needs?

If your answer to this question is "I'm not sure…" then consider choosing a hobby that involves others. There are lots of options. This could mean joining a group or team. You could take lessons or attend a class. Use your imagination.

Ask yourself, "Is there anything on my WishList that involves meeting and interacting with other like-minded people?"

A number of years ago, I took a series of private painting lessons. Eventually, I switched over to a group class. I wanted to see different perspectives, meet other painters, and gauge my progress. I really enjoyed both settings, and quickly determined the professionals out there were safe: selling paintings wasn't going to pay my mortgage.

If you already have the social connection you need, then pursue something on your own. Instead of searching out a local teacher or class to learn a new skill, maybe online is the way to go. A self-directed path is great for people who have enough social interaction and like going at their own pace.

GET OUT

Would leaving the house be good for you?

My whole concept of how to live your marathon and have happy retirement hinges upon building yourself a Plan to meet your needs, supported by the 2 Ps, Passion and Purpose. Having a hobby or two (or three) as part of the regular Steps you take almost guarantees you will get enough of the first P that keeps you young.

If you're someone who never leaves their home, then maybe picking a hobby requiring you to do so is a wise choice.

Likewise, if you're someone who's always out and about and on the go, maybe consider a quieter, do-it-at-home type of hobby as a counterbalance.

EXAMPLES FROM OTHERS

The other day I met with Susie, who's in her sixties. She told me she was really looking forward to learning how to play golf when she retired.

"Great," I said. "Do you have any idea how you're going to go about it?"

"Oh, heavens, yes," she replied. "I found a great deal online for seniors. I signed up for a package of eight group lessons at a public course around the corner from my house. I can't wait. It sounds like so much fun. It's two lessons a week. Each lesson is two hours long. The first hour we learn from an instructor and practice. Then, for the second, we go out on the course and play. And the cool part is the class is only for beginners, so everyone will be at my level."

"It's pretty obvious you're excited," I said. "You've got something new to learn and someplace to be twice a week for the next month. That's good."

"I even talked a friend into signing up too. We're going to meet new people we can golf with after we finish the lessons. And if we don't, at least we've got each other."

MEL'S (BEATLE) MANIA

Some people like to collect things. My lifelong friend, Mel, is one such person. He's been a Beatles fan from the beginning, gathering anything and everything Beatles since the invasion began when we were kids.

Eventually, as an adult, Mel became the national sales manager for a large company. This meant he spent his entire career on the road. One of his favorite things to do during his travels was to search out interesting Beatles paraphernalia to add to his collection. Usually this amounted to visiting used record stores and garage sales when he had the time.

A couple of years ago, Linda and I ran into Mel and his wife, Elaine, at a local restaurant. He had recently retired and was very excited to finally be off the road. I asked him about his retirement plans and he lit up.

"The first thing I'm going to do is organize my Beatles collection. Gary, you and Linda have to come over and check it out. You won't believe how much it's grown."

"I'm sure you'll love our basement full of dusty boxes..." Elaine was quick to add.

Mel gave her a look and said he'd be in touch. Sure enough, about three months after we ran into each other, he reached out.

To be honest, after Elaine's comment I was a bit skeptical and prepared for the worst. Boy, was I wrong...

Mel's basement wasn't full of dusty boxes at all. It was a full-on shrine to the Fab Four. It was awesome. The walls were plastered with posters, pictures, records, and magazines, some from other countries. It was a collection The Rock And Roll Hall of Fame would be proud to have.

Mesmerized, I asked, "Where did all of this come from?"

"I think my biggest score was at a garage sale in Kansas City. I was lucky enough to find a box labeled, 'Stuff from William.' Turns out, William was this guy's English pen pal. I about died when I opened it. It was stuffed with Beatles memorabilia from all over Europe."

"Mel, this is amazing! What's going to happen to all this when you and Elaine are gone?" I asked.

"The boys will get it. They're big Beatles fans too. And because I didn't want them to fight over any of it, there's a clause in my will stipulating how I want it to go. There's going to be a draft. I laid out the rules and everything."

TEACHING VIA TECHNOLOGY

One of my best friends, Harry, who hasn't retired yet, decided he wanted to learn how to play guitar. Instead of seeking out an instructor in person, Harry turned to YouTube. He typed "learn guitar" into the search bar and was amazed at how many videos came up. There were pages and pages of options.

Harry started at the top of the list. He watched it for a bit, but the teacher didn't really grab him. So, he moved on to a different instructor. Eventually, he found one he liked and reached out. Now, Harry and his digital guitar guru meet for weekly lessons over Skype.

Recently, about ten of us were at his house for happy hour. After multiple drinks, Harry brought out his guitar. My first thought was, "Oh, no." I had a flashback to being in college at Miami University and listening to a guy from my dorm play the worst version of "Fixing A Hole" I've ever heard. To my pleasant surprise and his credit, Harry nailed it.

I told him next time I'd be sure to bring my bongos.

AN EXCUSE TO EXERCISE

Is physical activity something you feel you need? If so, have you thought about playing pickleball?

If you're like me, maybe this suggestion has you scratching your head. "And what, exactly, is pickleball?" you ask. It's more or less a cross between tennis and badminton and chances are, there are people playing it near you. It's taking the retired world by storm.

I wasn't familiar with the game before chatting with a friend who used to play serious tennis. She had loved playing it up until the game stopped loving her back. When her body quit cooperating, tennis quit being fun. But her love for the game itself never wavered.

Then she discovered pickleball. It was love at first set. Now, she's able to use the skills she developed over her lifetime of playing tennis, only with much less physical strain on her body. As a bonus, she joined a mixed league, which led to her meeting all sorts of new people, including her new gentleman-friend.

She wanted a social, physical hobby to get her out of the house and force her to move around. Pickleball checked those boxes. And because of her history with tennis, she shortened the learning curve that accompanies trying new things.

ONE OF THE STRANGEST I'VE HEARD

Ross, a longtime client, introduced me to another unique hobby. He was about to retire when we met. And as you might have guessed, I asked him one of my go-to questions.

"Ross, what's the first thing you're going to do when you retire?"

Without missing a beat, he beamed, "I'm going to Costco."

Now, I've had clients tell me they were going to Disney World with the same level of excitement and enthusiasm, but Costco? Never. He wasn't kidding, though. That was his answer.

"Costco is the best," he said. "Have you ever been?"

"No, can't say I have."

"You've got to go, Gary, it's so cool. Right now, I'm thinking I'll end up going there at least twice a week when I retire. I'll stop by and pick you up on one of my trips."

Again, he was serious.

"I don't always find things I want to buy," he said. "But the food samples are great and there's something about wandering around this massive store I really enjoy. Every time I go, I find something I haven't seen before. It's fun."

I'm not a shopper, so this sounded more like punishment than pleasure to me, but for Ross, it was retail therapy heaven. And that's the point. Ross's retirement isn't mine. He probably thinks writing books and banging on bongos sound like torture.

POSSIBILITIES

Hopefully, one of the stories or an item on your WishList sparked something and inspired you to pursue a new hobby. If not, I threw together a list of potential hobbies you can try.

Sports/games: Pickleball, bowling, bocci, golf, skiing, cycling, swimming, card or board games.

The nice thing about picking up a sport or game is it leads to social connections. New friendships are healthy and not always easy to make. But a sport or game gives you a common ground to connect with people who you may like and want to spend more time with.

The arts/crafts: Drawing, coloring, painting, sculpting, building models, photography, musical instruments, carving wood, knitting.

I have one client whose favorite thing to do in his retirement is build dollhouses out of empty shotgun shells. He's a hunter who used to make dollhouses for his daughters when they were young. One day, he decided to put his two passions together.

Today, all four of his granddaughters have shotgun shell dollhouses. They're incredible. The last time he came to see me at the office, he brought one to show me. I swear it weighed more than I do, it was massive.

Everyone who sees one of his dollhouses tells him they want to buy one and that he should start a business. His reply? "Why? I don't need money. This is fun and I want it to stay that way."

Learn a new skill: Pick up a new language, become an amateur scientist, study genealogy, start tinkering in the garage.

Many universities and colleges offer discounted or free classes to seniors. In my home state, anyone over 65 is allowed to audit a college class for free. This is definitely something worth looking into if learning is a retirement hobby you'd like to explore.

Start collecting: Matchbooks, wine, beer, stamps, coins, cigars, golf books, vinyl, vintage appliances, Beatles memorabilia, toasters, coffee makers, old coin banks, you name it.

Two tips when it comes to collecting: Collect something you care about. The stronger your positive associations to whatever you decide to collect, the better you'll feel as you spend time with your collection.

The second tip is a warning. Please only collect things you can afford. One of the saddest things I see is when someone makes perfectly good financial decisions on the way up the mountain, only to ruin it all during the marathon. Only collect what you can afford and don't ever try to get rich from your collection.

Because if, like young John, Paul, George, and/or Ringo, you want money, don't worry. We're going to cover that in the next chapter.

INSIGHTS

Remember, this is your retirement. Not mine. It's not your spouse's or your neighbors' or your friends'.

Your Plan can look however you want it to look. What matters is it's built upon the 2 Ps and meets all your needs.

Hobbies are a wonderful Recurring Step and should absolutely be part of your Plan. By their very nature, they're tied to Passion.

So, comb through your WishList. Find a hobby or two that speaks to you and get going.

Don't be scared. You're allowed to test drive your hobbies. Try them before you buy and commit long-term.

Likewise, quit when you feel like it. No one is grading you. If it's no fun, it's not what you thought it would be, or you simply don't like it—stop.

Be careful, though. Frustration is a part of learning. Whether it's a new skill, a language, an instrument, or anything, really—expect it to be hard. Especially in the beginning. It's normal for new things not to come naturally or easily. Unless you're like my pickleball pal who played tennis her whole life and associated skills cross over.

When in doubt, you can always go back to your WishList and pick a new hobby. That's what it's there for.

Promise kept. At the beginning of this chapter, I said I'd refrain from using the "w" word, you know—the one that made Maynard G. Krebs squeak out loud on *The Many Loves of Dobie Gillis*—until the next chapter. Well, I hope you enjoyed the break. Because you'll be seeing plenty of that word starting now.

CHAPTER 24

Part-Time Jobs

ANY GUESSES AS TO the best Recurring Step to meet the needs you used to fill with work?

That's right. Going back to work.

The premise of this book is that meeting your needs in ways you enjoy leads to a successful retirement. And ironically, work is a really good way to meet many of those needs, so here we are. Let's run with this and see where it takes us…

This chapter is about making work "work" for you. On your terms. Not anyone else's.

Work, as you know, provides us with many things we need. Money is one of them. And if it's one of yours, then a part time job is a great way to supplement your income.

The same can certainly be said of structure. Each shift you work counts as a Step. Each Step equals a Win. Each Win is a reason to celebrate. I know celebrating work sounds strange, but you're really celebrating meeting your need for structure and getting in your Steps for the day.

Social connections are no different. Chances are a part-time job involves interacting with other people. Not always, but usually this is the case.

If it's self-worth you're lacking, a part-time job can help there too. As I've mentioned, there's usually a positive bump in self-esteem that accompanies earning money. Going back to work could be just what the doctor ordered.

RETIREMENT JOBS

When it comes to working part-time during your retirement, you have two main options. Option A involves continuing to work at your current job (or returning to it) in a reduced capacity. Option B is to start a new one.

I'm going to start with Option A for two reasons. First, because it's my favorite. Second, because so few people seem to believe it's viable.

OPTION A

I've seen this scenario play out in so many different, positive ways. It basically boils down to who's the boss.

Let's assume...

YOU'RE IN CHARGE

Here's what I want you to do...

1. **Go back to your Retirement Key**—Look over your Likes, Loves, and Hates.

2. **Handoff your Hates**—Delegate these tasks to someone who'd be good at them and enjoys them. Is there an employee who's sharp and eager for more responsibility? Could this person take on your Hates? You might have to give them a raise, but wouldn't it be worth it?

(By the way—the answer to the last question is always an emphatic, "Hell yes!")

3. **If that person doesn't exist, find them**—Hire someone new to take on these responsibilities. Surrounding yourself with competent people who actually like doing the stuff you hate makes life easier, better, and less stressful.

4. **If cost is your concern, take a page from history**—Think back to Part 1 and the history of retirement. Remember how pensions originally worked? Companies used to take half of a retiree's salary and use it to hire their replacement. Well, since you've reduced your workload from full-time to part-time, it may make sense for you to adjust your wages as well. Use the savings to increase the wages of the existing employee you found or to hire a new one. Freeing yourself from the weight of your Hates is well worth the costs.

5. **Use your imagination**—Create a new position. Design it specifically so you only do your Loves and Likes. Then, the hours you work will be pleasurable and full of your first P, Passion.

YOU'RE NOT IN CHARGE

Believe me, I recognize that not everyone reading this is the boss of their company. However, just because you're not the person making all the decisions doesn't mean my scaling-back approach won't work. Not only is there a good chance it will, but it's also liable to be a win-win for both you and the company.

A few years back, I met with Mark, a long-time client and friend.

"Gary," he said, "This year, I'm retiring."

"That's exciting, Mark. Any idea what your retirement is going to look like?" I asked.

"You got me. Maybe consult?"

"Consulting's a great gig," I replied. "How long have you been in the industry for? Thirty to thirty-five years? I'm sure you'll be an asset to any company hiring you. Have you mentioned any of this to the owner of your company? She might be interested."

"I seriously doubt Kathleen would be interested."

"Mark, as my dad used to say, 'You don't know what you don't know until you ask.' Unless you ask her, you're guessing. Set up a meeting with her. See what she thinks."

Mark didn't say anything. Clearly, by the look on his face, this was not a line of reasoning he'd ever imagined. My suggestion was being digested.

"Hmmmm...maybe you're onto something, Gary. We don't really have anyone part time, but Kathleen has brought in consultants for special projects before. She and I do work well together...and I do have a specialized skillset..."

"You're good at what you do," I told him. "Why not keep doing it there? Only do a little less of it and do it on your time instead of theirs."

"You think Kathleen would go for it?" he asked.

"Who knows? But one thing's for certain, asking her is the only way you'll ever find out."

About ten days later, I got a phone call.

"Hey, Gary! It's Mark. How's it going? I just wanted to call to say that you might be the smartest person I know."

Who doesn't love a call starting like that?

I laughed. "Mark, you really need to meet more people."

It was Mark's turn to laugh.

"No, Gary. I mean it. I sat down with Kathleen like you suggested, and it went better than I could have dreamed. I told her what I was thinking about consulting and mentioned your idea. She absolutely loved it. She told me she's actually been worried about me retiring and taking all my know-how with me when I go."

"Mark, that's wonderful news! I thought she might go for it."

"You were right. Kathleen was so excited. She and I started floating ideas of what my consulting could look like. I've got to tell you, it sounds perfect. I'll be working three days a week, Monday through Wednesday, and then have four days off. I can't wait. I almost want to retire now so I can start my new schedule, but I promised her I'd stay through the year."

BE LIKE MARK

This story isn't as unique as you might think. The truth is, you've spent years working at your company, learning the ins and outs, and perfecting what you do. This means you've got an incredible amount of knowledge—knowledge your company probably doesn't want to lose.

The chances a new employee will have your expertise and skillset is next-to-none. This fact alone puts you in better shape than you might think when it comes to negotiating. The more specialized your job, the more integral your contribution is to the overall success of your company. The more integral you are, the more leverage you have.

From your company's perspective, they want operations to continue as normal after you're gone. The trouble is, it's hard for it to be "business as usual" unless someone is doing all the little things you usually do. Many of which, I'm guessing, aren't in the training manual.

Offering to work part-time or to train your replacement is one way to ease into your retirement. It's a chance to make a few extra bucks and to get your feet wet experimenting with your Plan before jumping all-in.

So, if you like your job and working part-time is something you're leaning toward, be like Mark. Talk to the higher ups at your company. Remember my dad's adage: "You don't know what you don't know until you ask."

The worst that happens is you ask, and the answer is, "No." At which point, it's on to Option B.

OPTION B—GREENER PASTURES

Having almost finished this book, I hope you realize when I say "greener" I mean "greener for you." Retirement, as you know, isn't one-size-fits-all.

Before sharing my ideas about finding part-time work, there's something I'd like to clear up. The idea that businesses don't want to hire retirees is not always true.

Hiring retirees is smart business. One reason is employee benefits. Health insurance is expensive. However, people over 65 are eligible for Medicare. Medicare supplements are significantly less expensive than traditional health insurance. This saves employers money.

Next, retirees know what it means to have a job and work. They're dependable and responsible—qualities valued by employers. Today, absenteeism in the workforce is a serious problem. I don't know if you've noticed, but it's pretty difficult to run a business when people don't show up for work.

Then, there's the issue of training. If you're retired, you already have a general sense of what you need to do to be successful at a job. You know how to talk to customers. You know how to behave while on the clock, etc.

While these skills may feel like second nature to you because you've been doing them for years and they're automatic, the truth is, you learned these skills throughout your career and have been using them ever since.

WHERE TO START

I bet some of you guessed it. It starts with your WishList and Retirement Key.

Is there something on your WishList that screams "part-time job?" If so, excellent.

Truthfully, your ideal part-time job staring you in the face on your WishList doesn't happen too often. It's great when it does, but it's not the norm. The more common approach to finding a good part-time job relies on your Retirement Key.

I stand by what I said at the beginning of the chapter. You want a job that includes as many of your Loves and Likes, and as few of your Hates, as possible.

In order to help you find that job, I've created an advanced technique combining three Tools from Part 2.

MASTER LEVEL EXERCISE

Mark this page. Flip back to my Retirement Key at the end of Chapter 11 in Part 2. Using me as an example, it's pretty easy to see being a property manager or handyman would be terrible choices. I'd be horrible at them. And more importantly, they'd be horrible for me.

Same goes for anything even remotely dealing with technology. "Fixing things" and "Technology" are Hates of mine. There's zero chance I would enjoy a part-time job built around either of these two activities.

With "Music" and "Books" as Loves of mine, a part-time job in a bookstore or a record shop has potential.

Now, look at your own Retirement Key. With your particular Likes, Loves, and Hates, what sort of part-time jobs would be good for you? Get creative.

Unfortunately, without having your Retirement Key in front of me, I can't be much help with specifics. But fear not. Combining the suggestions and stories ahead with some old-fashioned brainstorming will give you plenty of ideas.

Ideally, you want to find a part-time job that marries your Passion and Purpose, the two pillars all good Plans need, and your Retirement Key.

By cross-referencing your Passions and your Purpose with jobs allowing you to be in your Likes and Loves, you further refine your list of good-fitting jobs. Then, if we're lucky, there will be a couple of options sitting in the sweet spot at the center, where all your circles overlap. These are jobs you would enjoy in industries or fields you're drawn to.

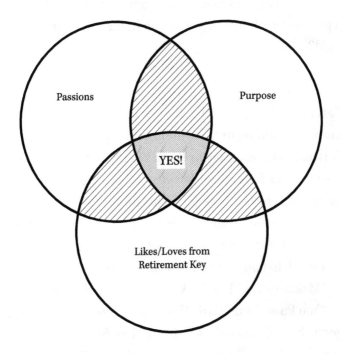

In case you're still confused, I've got some stories to share.

NOTICE NADIA

One of my clients, Nadia, retired and started working part-time at Lowes. She couldn't be happier. In her former work life, Nadia was a logistics coordinator for a large distribution company. She was the person in charge of making sure things got where they needed to be on time.

Now, she works in the receiving department. She went from being the one responsible for sending products to the one who receives them. Finding herself on the other side of the supply chain is something she enjoys.

Is there a page you can take from Nadia's book? Is there a part-time job that interests you in the same, or a related field?

COPY CARL

Carl is another person I'd like you to meet. He and I didn't know one another until we literally bumped into each other. We were both reaching for the baked brie on the hors d'oeuvre table at a fundraiser. Between bites of delicious puffed pastry and cheese, I asked, "What do you do?"

"Oh, I've been retired from being a real estate appraiser for almost twenty years," he said. "But I learned quickly I was much happier when I had something to do."

"Makes sense," I said. "What did you end up doing?"

"You know," said Carl, "I was fortunate enough to be in good shape financially, so I focused on finding something I really enjoyed. I've been a lifetime baseball fan but never had the time to attend many games. It was February, spring training was about to start in Arizona, and I told my wife we should go. The way she looked at me, you'd have thought I suggested boarding a spaceship and heading to Mars."

"Arizona didn't end up happening, but in the course of talking about it, my wife made an off-hand comment, 'Maybe you can be one of those usher guys at the stadium.' Sure enough, they were hiring stadium personnel and I've been an 'usher guy' ever since."

I lit up. As you might have noticed, I'm a huge Cleveland sports fan. "Seriously? You work at the ballpark? That's incredible. I love baseball."

"Me too, thanks to my brother. He passed away a number of years ago, but, boy, did he love listening to games. He's the one who got me into baseball. It might sound a little strange, but when I'm at the stadium I feel connected to him. It's what I love most about my job. Well, that and the free parking."

So the question is: What speaks to you? What Passion? What hobby? Following your Likes and Loves to a part-time job could be your ticket. It would put you in contact with like-minded people and come with some perks.

By "perks" I mean the non-monetary benefits you'd receive from your job. It could be an employee discount on merchandise or services, or spending time in a particular setting. Perhaps, like for Carl, it's free parking. Whatever the added perk is, make sure it's valuable to you. Then it sweetens the deal.

Another way to go about finding a good-fitting part-time job is to follow Laura's lead.

LEARN FROM LAURA

Laura is a client of mine who retired from nursing. She spent her entire career working a very specific schedule: the grave-yard shift. And it turns out, after spending forty years working nights, adjusting to "bankers' hours" was a bit of a struggle.

One night, Laura went out to dinner. She and her friends were celebrating a birthday and wanted it to be special. This led them to eat at one of her friend's members-only club.

After the meal, as everyone was gathering their coats and saying their goodbyes, Laura noticed a sign. "Wanted: After hours cleaner. Inquire with the manager." She asked her friend, the one who was a member, to introduce her to the manager.

Laura started her new part-time job the next night.

"Gary," she said, "I love it. The job is so easy. The members all seem to take pride in their club so they take pretty good care of the place. The dining room closes at 11 p.m. I come in at midnight. No one else is usually there, so it's just me and my headphones. I put on some tunes and get to work."

"Wow, Laura. That sounds like a perfect fit," I said.

"It is. I finally feel like myself again. I'm back on my normal schedule and the manager couldn't be happier. I got a raise after the first month. Plus, she told me I could come in and eat dinner there a couple nights a week. Nothing wrong with free fancy food."

Are you the type of person who's been on a very specific schedule for as long as you can remember and don't feel like changing? There are jobs out there that'll allow you to stay in your Likes and Loves, and fit your *whens*.

Nadia, Carl, and Laura are three examples of different people who used different criteria to find good fitting part-time jobs. Nadia chose to work in a field adjacent to the one she used to work in. Carl became an usher because he had a passion for baseball. Laura started cleaning a restaurant because it worked well with her *when*. Each story offers you a different approach to finding part-time jobs.

STILL STUMPED?

I've had clients who have worked in grocery stores, drug stores, coffee shops, and every type of retail you can imagine. Recently, many clients started driving for Uber or Lyft. I know retired people who love golf and now work part-time at courses so they can play for free.

None of these jobs will make any of these people rich, but they all have upsides. They're excuses to be out of the house and interact with people. So, while no fortunes are likely to be made by working them, these part-time jobs are good for their bodies, minds, and souls.

Working part time is a Recurring Step that, at the very least, helps you meet your needs for social connection, money, and structure.

One friend of mine has switched part-time jobs three times in four years. She keeps trying different things, searching for the perfect fit. I saw her recently. She said she's found it.

"I saw an ad. A local college was looking for teachers. Now, I'm an adjunct professor. I love it. I get to interact with the students a couple days a week and pass along what I've learned."

Remember, the possibilities are nearly endless.

If you've been looking for the right part-time job but haven't found it yet, hang in there. Go back to your WishList and Retirement Key. Think about the examples in this chapter. Be patient. Something will click. Keep trying and give it time.

INSIGHTS

I'm a big fan of retirement jobs. They are a great addition to anyone's Pool. That's why this is one of the longest chapters in the book.

Part-time work can help meet your needs for social interaction, money, and structure. If you're lucky and smart, the list doesn't end there. Passion and Purpose can also be incorporated into your part-time job.

If Mark's story motivated you, and reducing yourself to a part-time position at your current or previous job is what you're after, then sit down with the decision makers and pitch the idea to them. Remember my dad's advice. "You don't know what you don't know until you ask."

If you're looking for a new and different job, then don't settle. Find something that allows you to operate in your Likes and Loves in a field you enjoy, harmonizes with your when, and offers meaningful perks.

Now, there's only one more type of Recurring Step left for us to cover. It's the single most effective and consistent way I've found to pile up as many Wins as you can. And it's also my favorite, which is why I saved it for last.

CHAPTER 25

Working for Free

VOLUNTEERING AND MENTORSHIP ARE what this chapter is all about. Because believe it or not, spending some of your hard-earned time working for free, after spending decades doing it for money, is a pretty solid move when it comes to retiring.

I know Chapter 14 was a while ago. In it, I defined purpose as what you do for others. Doing things for others out of the kindness of your heart is the definition of volunteering, which is why you should seriously consider adding it to your Pool of Steps. It all but guarantees the second pillar, Purpose, will be a part of your Plan.

In many ways, finding a good fit for volunteering is identical to finding a good fitting part-time job. Refer back to the previous chapter, specifically the section titled "Filter Through Your 2 Ps." With a subtle tweak, it becomes an exercise that works just as well for finding a good place to volunteer, just as it does for working part-time.

Before, when you used this Filter, you focused on the Likes and Loves from your Retirement Key. This was a Passion-centric approach. But now that we're talking about volunteering and mentorship, you'll want to make Purpose the focal point. So, instead of taking a full-stop at your Likes and Loves, you'll want to zero in on your Likes and Loves that help others.

Once those are front and center for you, it's about finding an opportunity to act on them. You want to stay in your Likes and Loves while volunteering and do it on your schedule. That's the sweet spot when working for free.

However, finding the perfect place to volunteer does not guarantee it's going to be a perfect fit. It's important to do a little investigating. Talk to the volunteer coordinator. Get a detailed description of what is involved.

This could prevent you from getting the worst kind of surprise. And unfortunately, that can happen when you show up to volunteer at a place you think perfectly blends your Passion and Purpose, only to have a mop shoved into your hands.

The rest of this chapter is my answer to the all-too-common concern I've heard countless times, "I'd love to volunteer. I just don't know where..."

CRAFTY CRAIG

One of Craig's Loves is working with his hands. Building and fixing things is one of his Passions. He's been retired for five years, and now spends three days a week at his church doing odd jobs and repairs.

This means each time Craig volunteers at his church, it's a triple Win. Going there is one of his Steps for the day. While he's there, he's doing one of his Loves. And he's doing it in service of someone else. Every time Craig volunteers at his church, it checks the boxes for his schedule, Purpose, and Passion.

This is what you want your retirement to look like.

LOOK AT LANIE

Lanie was a school teacher in her former work life. She retired last year and loves to be on the road.

"Gary," she told me at a meeting, "Driving is one of my favorite things to do in this world. I swear when I come back in my next life, I'll be a truck driver."

I could tell she wasn't kidding.

Lanie decided to use her love of driving to serve others. She volunteers with two different organizations. The first is Meals on Wheels. The second provides door-to-door service for people who need transportation to doctors' appointments, etc.

Between volunteering for both causes, Lanie is able to spend time (a Step) on the road (Passion) either delivering food to people or delivering people to places. Either way, she's helping others (Purpose). Much like Craig, Lanie has built herself a retired life that includes regular triple Wins to celebrate.

The last time she and I saw each other, she surprised me. "Gary, I think my favorite part of my volunteering has to do with the friends I've made."

"What do you mean?" I asked.

"A lot of the people I chauffeur are repeat customers. You can only spend so much time in a car with another person before you start talking and getting to know them. I've ended up becoming friends with almost everyone I drive."

"That's great!" I said.

"It is. It is," she paused. "Except now, we're always stopping for lunch."

"Doesn't sound too bad."

"Gary, you don't understand. Everyone I drive likes their desserts. I've never eaten so much ice cream in my entire life."

POSSIBLE PLACES YOU CAN WORK FOR FREE

Schools—Two clients of mine help out at schools, doing radically different things. One spends his time at an elementary school running an after-school program, teaching the kids how to play chess. The other is a crossing guard. Both have added purpose and structure to their lives by taking Recurring Steps to help children.

Meals on Wheels or a local food bank—These are excellent ways to make a positive impact on the community. There is also a social component. Between those you're volunteering with and those you're serving, there's plenty of opportunity to interact with others.

Community gardens—Volunteering here means spending time out of the house and in nature. Most gardeners I know love their hobby and look for almost any excuse to go out and do it. As an added bonus, if it's food you're growing, you can donate the actual fruits and vegetables of your labors to benefit food needs in your community.

Races—Be it a 5K, a marathon, a triathlon, or bike race, it doesn't matter. The organizers all need help. Races are huge productions requiring lots of willing people. Volunteering at a race puts you in touch with your community. It also allows you to make a difference in the lives of complete strangers as they challenge their physical limits.

Hospitals or Hospice—If caring for people is something you enjoy, one of these places might be for you. A friend of mine holds premature babies at a local hospital once a week. Another friend spends time at a local Hospice center helping the families of the patients. When I last saw him, he told me it might be the most rewarding thing he's ever done.

Museums—Have you always enjoyed Art? History? Science? Is there a museum close to you specializing in something you're interested in? Reach out. Ask if they need help. You may be pleasantly surprised.

National, State, or Local parks—If you're the type of person who's always enjoyed being in nature, then contact your local parks district and see what you can do to pitch in.

Sports—Love sports? Either playing them or helping others play them? Contact a local youth or recreational league. Schools are another place you can touch base with to see if they need help. Perhaps you can help the coach, run the scoreboard, keep stats, work concessions, or coordinate logistics.

Youth Centers—Contact YMCAs or YWCAs, or any local community center, for that matter. Again, spending time with young people and helping them can be a positive investment of your free time.

Local Events—Where I live, there's always some sort of event going on. Look at the newspaper. Pull up a community calendar online, or check in with your Chamber of Commerce to see what's coming up and sounds fun.

Political Organizations or Nonprofits—If you're passionate about a specific cause and there's a national organization with a local chapter around you, you can help them.

Rotary—This one surprised me. I never thought I'd be a Rotary member but turns out I was wrong. I enjoy the meetings. Through Rotary, I stay in touch and involved with my community. Every Friday between 11:30 a.m. and 1:30 p.m., I know I'll be eating lunch with friends and listening to an interesting speaker.

BUT MY ABSOLUTE FAVORITE WAY TO VOLUNTEER IS...

Mentoring is my absolute favorite way to volunteer. As a guy who loves Wins (which I'm sure you've noticed by now), I'm not sure there's a better way to get them, at least not for me.

"Helping others," "Sharing what I've learned," and "Solving problems" are Loves of mine. These are Passions. So, every time I mentor someone, it's a three-Win Step.

But wait, there's more. Because the actual activity of being a mentor—sitting down with someone and working with them—also meets my needs for social interaction and identity/value/worth. For those of you counting at home, that's five Wins.

Talk about a powerful Recurring Step you can take. I honestly don't think there's a better one. At least, not if your goal is to retire and be happy.

Go out and find someone who needs help. Give one of the greatest gifts you can. Pass along the wisdom and experience you've gained throughout your life and help someone else succeed.

REAL WORLD EXAMPLES

While attending a Rotary meeting, I sat next to a woman who had recently retired. She was the president of an accounting firm. Waiting for the meeting to start, I struck up a conversation.

"So, how's retired life?" I asked.

"Honestly? I'm so bored. One day, I was the president of a large firm and the next day I wasn't. People used to ask me questions and my opinion mattered. Now? No one asks me anything. I miss solving problems and feeling important. This retirement thing has been a massive hit to my self-esteem."

"I'm sorry," I said. I appreciate you being honest. Not many people are as candid about what they're going through."

"It's been a real struggle. In a strange way, I feel like I'm wasting away. There's not much stimulation in my life anymore. It's depressing."

"Have you ever thought of becoming a mentor?"

She was about to respond, but the crack of the gavel beat her to it. The meeting started before we could finish our conversation.

About a month later, she and I ended up sitting next to each other again. This time she started the conversation.

"Gary, thank you so, so much. I don't know if you remember, but a while back we chatted. I was struggling with being retired and you told me to look into becoming a mentor. Well, I took your advice and I've got to tell you—I am so excited."

"That's great," I said. "What happened?"

"I got in touch with my old colleagues and asked them if they knew of anyone who could use some guidance. Three days later, I received an email from an intern at my old firm. She and I have our first face-to-face meeting tomorrow. Gary, this is going to be fun."

I could tell by the smile on her face she was telling the truth.

Here's a second example.

I met a young man who wants to start a photography business. He's a barista at one of the coffee shops I frequent and he's about to graduate from high school.

It was a slow day so we were able to spend a good ten or fifteen minutes talking. I listened to him tell me about the type of business he wanted to start. When he was done, I offered my thoughts and some advice.

Since our initial conversation, this young man and I have crossed paths many times. Each time we do, he tells me about the steps he's taking and challenges he's facing.

Sharing in his successes, setbacks, and progress has been incredibly rewarding for me. In fact, I think I enjoy being a part of his journey even more than the mochas he makes. And he makes a mean mocha.

FINDING SOMEONE TO MENTOR

Is there anyone in your world who could benefit from your years of experience and wisdom?

Think about it.

If the answer is "Yes" then reach out. See if they're interested.

If no one comes to mind, or the person you thought might be a candidate isn't, don't be discouraged. There are resources available to help you find the person you're looking for.

Most local colleges and high schools offer business classes. Reaching out to these programs and departments is one way of finding someone to mentor. Organizations like the Small Business Association and the Chamber of Commerce are other sources for possible candidates.

Going to www.score.org is another. This is a website designed to match mentors with small business owners who are seeking assistance.

You've got an amazing skillset—one you've spent a lifetime building. Everything you've done. Everything you've been through. Everything you've learned. There's a good chance there are people working in your field, or similar ones, who are just starting out and could benefit from your experience and wisdom.

Mentor someone. Pass along what you've learned. Help someone else. Help yourself. Because ultimately, that's what will happen when you decide to spend some hard-earned retired time working for free. You'll have a happier and longer retirement.

INSIGHTS

Retiring and not dying means meeting your needs.

These needs include but are not limited to: structure, identity/value/worth, social connection, passion, and purpose.

Volunteering is a single Step you can take to meet them all. One Step. Just ONE!

That's why I'm such a huge fan of making volunteering, and specifically mentorship, a part of your retirement Plan. To my knowledge, there isn't a more powerful or potent Recurring Step you can take. It's a guaranteed three to five Wins every time you do it.

Wow. It feels like only yesterday we started our journey together. And now look at you. About ready to go off on your own and live your marathon and the happy, retired life of your dreams...

Alright, you turn the page. I'm going to make a mocha. And we'll meet in the next chapter, which is also our last.

CHAPTER 26

Pick Out Your Steps

"PICK OUT YOUR STEPS. Uh-huh. Pick out your Steps. Alright."

I've loved Average White Band ever since I saw them live at Tangier's in Akron, Ohio.

In fact, their track, "Pick Up the Pieces," the one I named this last chapter after (with a little spin), is one of my all-time favorite celebration songs. There's so much joy and good energy oozing out of all the horns, it seeps into my soul every time I hear it. Which is fitting because we have plenty to celebrate.

And I do mean we. You've made it to the end of my book, learning along the way what it takes to stay young and retire successfully. As for me, I've successfully finished writing my third book.

But before I go down the street to get my hot fudge milkshake and you go off to do whatever it is you like to do to celebrate your Wins, one thing remains...

BUILDING YOUR PLAN

Since the beginning of the book and the story of Bruno and

Betty, I've been telling you again and again, you need a Plan in order to have a happy and successful retirement. Every chapter has reinforced this message. And now, it's finally time for you to build your Plan.

You've done the groundwork.

You've learned to use your Tools.

You know your needs and natural rhythms.

You have some ideas about what kind of Steps you want to take.

Now, it's time to put together everything we've been talking about and have a little fun.

Because honestly, if you can't have fun building your Plan—the very thing providing you the retirement of your dreams—then what's the point?

There's no time like the present. Let's get this train rolling.

PRIORITIZE

YOUR NATURAL HOURS + YOUR NEEDS = YOUR MOST IMPORTANT STEPS.

Since you're in charge of your time, you're aware of your natural rhythms, and you know your needs—you are the expert. There isn't another person on the planet better equipped to build your Plan than you.

A night owl who loves sports and is looking to be more social will have different needs than someone who's up with the sun and wants a part-time job to earn some extra cash. What's important is staying between the lines of your unique situation. That's how you choose the right Steps.

Once you've got Steps covering the bases of your needs, it's time to choose ones to meet...

YOUR WANTS

With Steps scheduled to meet your needs, it's time to take care of your wants. After all, this is your retirement. This is why you spent thirty or forty years climbing the mountain of employment. Make it count.

Make your marathon one with plenty of the first P. Everything you do for yourself is Passion, and that's something you need to stay young. This means spending as many Steps as you can on hobbies, skills, and things piquing your interest.

Remember your Retirement Key. Do as many of your Likes and Loves as you can.

Don't forget your WishList. This Tool is full of your wants. That's why you made it. Use it to help you choose your Steps.

Spending time with your friends is another excellent Step to add to your days. Reach out. See if someone's doing something fun and wants company. Or invite someone along to join you when you do an activity you think they might enjoy.

Another Step I'd be remiss not to mention again is celebrating your Wins. Whatever this means to you, whether it's going out to a nice dinner, staying in for an afternoon to read, or anything in between, C-E-L-E-B-R-A-T-E. Do so in meaningful and responsible ways.

Before sending you off into the sunset of the retirement of your dreams, I want to take a moment to answer some of the more common questions you might have.

Q&A

Q.—What sort of balance should I strike between Recurring and Once-in-a-while Steps?

A.—That depends entirely on you. Personally, I like a ⅔, ⅓ split between the two. Having two Recurring Steps and a Once-in-a-while Step provides the balance I like. It gives me the consistency and variety I need.

However, my friend, Doug, is the exact opposite. He gets bored easily and that's a slippery slope toward depression for him. But Doug knows this. He's aware he's a happier person when he stays active and keeps moving in new directions. Doug does everything in his power to avoid taking the same Step two days in a row.

Q.—How many different Steps do I need to have in any given week?

A.—3 Steps a day adds up to twenty-one Steps per week. The range you want to shoot for is probably somewhere between twelve to eighteen total. Folks like Doug on the other hand, may need more. Again, it's your retirement. You know yourself and your needs better than anyone else. Build your Plan accordingly.

Q.—Gary, I've read your book. I've tried your system and it's not working. What am I doing wrong?

A.—Ah, to you, dear reader, I'd say be sure to read the conclusion. There's a delicious, cool, refreshing answer waiting for you there.

Choosing your Steps is more art than science. It starts with being aware of your needs. Next, it's about figuring out what the best Steps are, the best time to take them, and doing them.

Be creative. Use all your Tools. Take your time. Think smart. The more Steps you can come up with to meet multiple needs at once, the more time you'll have to focus on your wants. This all but guarantees your Plan has enough of your first pillar, Passion.

If you're stumped and need a little guidance, re-read Part 3.

When in doubt, or in need of another Step to round out your day, remember to celebrate. Every Win is worthy of a celebration. Every celebration can be a Step.

That's it. That's what I know. I have given you everything I've learned in my forty-plus years of helping people retire and not die.

I wish you all the best, and many, many, many happy, successful, wonderful miles in your marathon.

All I ask is when someone says, "What's your secret? You're the happiest retired person I know," think about the beginning of this book. Remember, Purpose is a P you need, and help them by becoming their Retirement Role Model.

Above all, enjoy living your marathon. Because that's what it's all about.

CONCLUSION

BEFORE SENDING YOU OFF on your merry way to live your marathon, there's one last story I'd like to share. While it's true the drinks I've talked about the most are milkshakes and mochas (I guess I've got a thing for chocolate and the letter "M"), over the past year another beverage has become one of my Likes: "Old-fashioneds."

Linda and I have never been big drinkers. If you saw our liquor cabinet, you'd laugh. There are bottles in there that are older than my son, Max. He's 40.

But one night we were out to dinner with our friends, Rob and Beth, and Rob ordered one. On a whim, I decided to do the same. After the first sip, I realized drinking old-fashioneds is an acquired taste, which miraculously I acquired by the time I finished my first one.

On our way out of the restaurant, I decided to stop by the bar and compliment Eric, the bartender, on his cocktail. He smiled and said thanks, not taking his eyes off the martini he was shaking.

"Hey, by the way, how do you make one of those old-fashioneds?" I asked.

Without looking up from the drink he was pouring, Eric rattled off his recipe in rapid fire. I swear there were seventeen steps. When Eric finally did look up, he laughed. Seeing I had not comprehended his speedy delivery, Eric grabbed a slip of paper and scribbled the recipe down. I dropped a five dollar bill in his tip jar and said "Thank you."

The next afternoon I took his recipe and headed to the grocery store with Eric's list in hand.

On my way out of the house, Linda assured me we had sugar I could use to make simple syrup, and I could use her pestle for muddling. I'm guessing it was the blank expression on my face that caused her to laugh. I had no idea what she was talking about.

There were only four things on the list I needed from the store—bourbon, bitters, cherries, and an orange. As a guy who likes to get easy Wins and build momentum, I started with the citrus.

Orange in hand, I made my way to the liquor section thinking to myself, "This shouldn't be too hard. After all, how many different kinds of cherries, bitters, and bourbon can there be?"

The answer was: a lot. I was floored. Thank God for the woman working there. After my third lap through the aisles, she very sweetly walked over and asked if I could use some help.

"Thank you," I said, "I'm looking for bourbon, bitters, and cherries. I've walked around here three times and I can't seem to find any of these. I would love some help."

She smiled. "Making old-fashioneds? Let's start with the whiskey," she said.

If it wasn't for the very nice lady working that day, I might still be in the liquor store trying to decide between the grapefruit-infused bitters or the Peychaud's. Same goes for the whiskey. And the cherries.

Returning home, I set about the task of making Eric's recipe. I knew I needed a chilled glass, so the first thing I did was put one in the freezer. I also knew I needed a bit of orange peel. Luckily, having peeled plenty of potatoes in my youth, this time at least I knew what I was looking for.

Linda was kind enough to set out the pestle, a strainer, the sugar, a measuring cup, a pot, and the whisk. So I started making the simple syrup, learning quickly why it was called that. It's just water and sugar. Who knew?

Feeling confident, I grabbed a glass. I threw one of the Luxardo cherries into the bottom, splashed in some bitters, added the orange peel, and a little ice. Having never done this before and not knowing any better, the glass I grabbed was, in fact, made of glass and had a thin bottom. This was a bad choice.

I think it might have been my third or fourth mash when I broke the glass, "Shit!" I yelled, more out of surprise than disgust. Shaking my head, taking a breath, and exhaling deeply, I laughed at myself, cleaned up the broken glass, and started over.

This time, I grabbed a thicker glass and used a lot less intensity. It was a good strategy. By the time I finished muddling, my simple syrup was ready to go and my glass was properly chilled.

"Now we're cooking," I thought.

Next, I added the simple syrup, followed by the Makers Mark the nice lady recommended, and then I gave my concoction a couple swirls for good measure. Satisfied, I grabbed the glass from the freezer, added some ice to it, and used the strainer to pour myself my first-ever homemade old-fashioned.

I was proud of myself and excited. "This is gonna be so good..." I thought as I took my first sip.

As soon as it hit my tongue I started laughing. I did a full-on spit take, coughing my cocktail all over the kitchen counter. It was awful.

I don't know if I used too much sugar when I made my simple syrup, or if I simply added too much. Either way, it was entirely too sweet to drink. And this is coming from a guy who might be addicted to milkshakes and mochas.

With a heavy sigh, I dumped what I thought was going to be a delicious old-fashioned down the drain. Deflated but not defeated, I grabbed three glasses to put in the freezer, just in case. After cleaning up my latest mess, I took another crack at it.

My second old-fashioned was absolutely better than my first, but in reality, the bar was quite low. It also ended up down the drain. My third one was undrinkable and the worst attempt by far. I think I may have gotten carried away with the bitters. But my fourth one? Jackpot.

It was a clone of Eric's masterpiece.

Excited and proud, I went outside to find Linda in her garden. "Here, try this," I said, handing her the glass.

She took a sip. Her eyes lit up. "Wow," she said. "I'm really impressed. I can't believe you nailed it on your first try."

INSIGHTS

I wanted to share this last story with you to illustrate a very important lesson. In Part 1, you read a chapter about the Retirement Mindset. And, since it was a while ago, I thought a refresher might be in order.

People don't generally do well at complicated tasks the first time they try them. However, a little levity, humor, persistence, and determination can go a long way to figuring it out in the end. It took me four tries, one broken glass, two kitchen messes, and maybe seventy-five minutes to make a cocktail I could actually drink and enjoy.

Remember me and my old-fashioneds when you're building your Plan. The task you're setting out to do isn't an easy one. Retirement, like life, is complicated. It has a lot of moving parts.

This means you may have your fair share of broken glasses, messes to clean up, and trial runs before you get it right. And when that happens, do what I did.

Say, "Shit!"

Laugh it off.

Pour your drink down the drain.

And start again.

Until you get it right.

ACKNOWLEDGMENTS

THIS BOOK HAS BEEN a family and friends affair. First off, my son Max and I co-wrote this book, and my wife, Linda, edited our words to make it a readable and worthwhile experience.

Thank you to my friend Dan Sullivan, founder of Strategic Coach (www.strategiccoach.com), for inspiring me to write books.

To Don Harbert for his coaching expertise.

To my friends who volunteered to read and critique my book—David and Terry Katz, Bill and Candy Wallace, Diane and Bill Blocker, Barry Adelman, Christy Allensworth, David Herbert, and Maria Schepis.

Thank you to Gino Wickman (www.e-leap.com) for his book writing suggestions and sage advice.

A big thank you to the employees at Sirak Financial Services—Jeffrey Sirak, Raquel Thompson, Linda Smith, Lisa Fleming, Tara Gordon, Jennifer Cassidy, Mackenzie Jeffers, Nicole Baldwin, Kelly Presson, Matt DiRuzza, Thomas Houston, and Chris Groubert for their support and encouragement throughout the entire process.

Thanks to Charlie Epstein for our title discussion at Strategic Coach.

Thank you to Ryan Humbert, lead singer of the Shootouts, for his graphics and cover design.

Thank you to Alex Dowell at Five Arrows Marketing for her marketing skills and creating the *Friday Morning Coffee with Gary* series on YouTube.

Thank you to my friend, Mike Galina, for his *Friday Morning Coffee with Gary* conversations.

Thank you to Shannon Waller for her suggestions and encouragement.

Thanks to The Steve Harrison Group for helping to promote my book.

Thanks to the Scribe team for putting it all together. Your talented staff was great to work with and very professional.

(Max would like to sneak some thanks in here too…To his mom and dad, thanks for raising me, and for being the editor and the brains behind this whole book, respectively. To STS9 who, unbeknownst to them, provided the soundtrack for the final draft. And of course, to the readers. Anyone who's made it this far deserves a whole host of thanks. It was all for you.)

CPSIA information can be obtained
at www.ICGtesting.com
Printed in the USA
LVHW080840071021
699808LV00003B/100/J

9 781544 523743